TROUT & SALMON FISHING
IN
NORTHERN NEW ENGLAND

TROUT & SALMON FISHING
IN
NORTHERN NEW ENGLAND

A Guide to Selected Waters in Maine, New Hampshire, Vermont and Massachusetts

by

Al Raychard

NORTH COUNTRY PRESS

THORNDIKE, MAINE

Library of Congress Cataloging in Publication Data:

Raychard, Al.
  Trout & salmon fishing in northern New England.

  1. Trout fishing—New England—Guide-books.
  2. Salmon fishing—New England—Guide-books.
  3. Fishing—New England—Guide-books.
I. Title. II. Title: Trout and salmon fishing in northern New England.
SH688.U6R38 1982   **799.1′755**   **82-5930**
ISBN 0-89621-068-5 (pbk.)   **AACR2**

Cover design by Paul Loweree.

Special thanks to Tom Chamberlain of the Maine Department of Inland Fisheries and Wildlife, Augusta, Maine.

Photos by Al Raychard.

Again to Sandra, and as always, with love.

CONTENTS

TROUT & SALMON FISHING
IN
NORTHERN NEW ENGLAND

FOREWORD

The rivers and streams of northern New England are unique resources. From the native brook trout streams of Maine, to the Battenkill of Vermont, to the brownie-infested waters of the Deerfield in the Berkshires of western Massachusetts, we fly fishing enthusiasts have at our doorsteps some of the finest trout and salmon flowages east of the Mississippi.

I have heard it said that few of New England's waters have the ability to produce what many call "high quality" fishing. But I have always thought that any river or stream capable of supporting trout or salmon, and that can produce a marginal hatch of may flies or caddis flies, and is clean, is worthy of this "high quality" label. Even in this day and age, when miles and miles of running water in other areas of the country are being lost daily to pollution, dams, and other alterations, many of the streams and rivers in northern New England still meet the criteria needed to support and sustain populations of coldwater fish.

I have often wondered why so many fishing enthusiasts desire to travel west to wet their lines and cast a fly. In truth, we have great sportfishing potential here in New England — many rivers of varied characteristics and insect life. And some impressive species to choose from, too. The salmon fly hatch on Montana's Madison River was truly a phenomenon to behold — and fish over. But even during my visit there, I was wondering about the salmon on the West Branch, and those Nesowadnehunk Stream brookies I love so well. I couldn't wait to get home — to travel to the "catch-and-release" area on the Deerfield, among other places. Fishing out west *is* magnificent, and I hope every fisherman who desires to go can make the trip at least once. But give me the trout and salmon streams of New England, and I'm happy.

I don't remember the first time I fished a river or stream for trout or salmon — it was some years ago. But I do remember the great fun I had, and the challenge of getting that first native brookie or landlock to accept my fly remains deeply embedded in my memory. Needless to say, I have been "hooked" on river and stream fishing ever since. Like most enthusiasts, I am astream every chance I get.

I didn't really get serious about fly fishing until after I left high school. By then I had heard of the West Branch, and I fished it for the first time the year of my graduation. I still visit that famed salmon river whenever I get the chance.

The Kennebago, the Roach, Grand Lake Stream, and eventually the Rapid, also became favorite weekend havens, and still are. Today I know them well, although at times I wonder whether we ever really know or understand a trout stream. But there was a time when I didn't understand any of them, which brings us to the reason for this book.

During my "novice days" of stream fishing, I would have sold my casting arm for just one concise, easy-to-read guide book to some of the better trout and salmon flowages of New England. Such a publication, I thought, would be immensely beneficial to novice — and visiting — fishermen in Maine, New Hampshire, Vermont, and Massachusetts, helping them locate the better pools and riffle areas on rivers such as the West Branch, the Kennebago, New Hampshire's upper Connecticut and Androscoggin rivers, or Vermont's Battenkill and Lamoille. Such a book, I thought, would be worth its weight in gold. But it never came, until now.

I wanted things easy, however. Not only did I want a book that showed the location of the productive pools and riffle sections. I also wanted that book to show me access roads and trails, and tell me the best time to fish a specific river. I wanted it to tell me the best flies to use, and offer information on places to lodge and camp. I wanted from this book anything that would help me in my quest for a memorable and successful fishing trip.

Well, as I said, such a book just never came off the presses. So much of my knowledge concerning the rivers and streams of northern New England came the hard way: by taking the time to visit, fish, and explore them — by fishing them at the wrong times, after the principal hatches had come and gone, or when water conditions were too high or too low. Looking back, I realize now that this was fun and most educational, and if I had to do it all over again, I probably would. But I still would have liked that guide book!

It is for primarily this reason that I decided to write this book. I remember well what I went through to find productive trout and salmon fishing on the streams and rivers of New England. And there are undoubtedly fishermen going through the same thing today. If you are, as I was, looking for a helpful guide to New England's trout and salmon waters, I believe you will find this one most helpful.

Much of the information and material in the following pages was obtained from personal experience. Every river or stream mentioned has been visited and fished personally sometime within the past few years, then revisited and refished for material for this book. While my impressions of a specific river, my suggested times to fish it, or the flies I recommend may not necessarily agree with those of enthusiasts who live near that river or know it exceedingly well, the information provided for each stream and river, which I collected during one or more visits, will hit the target, if not the bull's-eye.

I have not tried to teach "how to" fish a trout stream. I will leave that to other authors. What I hoped to do, and what I believe I have done, is to offer an easy-to-read guide book to some of the better trout and salmon flowages of northern New England, providing the best information available concerning their general descriptions and locations and best times to fish them, possible productive flies, and data on where to lodge or camp. This *is* that book I wanted and would have found helpful when I started out years ago. And if you find it so, then all the effort has been worthwhile.

AL RAYCHARD
August, 1981

Chapter 1

The States

MAINE

Sitting in the extreme northeastern corner of the United States, Maine is the largest state in New England, covering slightly more than 33,000 square miles. Generally, the land mass is heavily forested, with some agricultural land in each county. The southern counties are quite flat, this terrain changing to rolling hills as you travel westward to the New Hampshire border. But from the Rangeley Lake country northward and northeastward, the visitor will find the great "wilderness" region for which Maine is so famous.

The coastal plain, along with two interior counties (Kennebec and Androscoggin), are the most heavily populated, although there is at least one large city or town in each of the sixteen counties. Considering its size, Maine is very sparsely populated, with slightly more than one million citizens.

Tourism and outdoor-oriented activities and sports have always been, and will continue to be, major industries in Maine — the state is subsequently geared in those directions in many areas. Travel to nearly any area in the lower half of the state is not difficult; exceptions are certain sections in the western and northern counties. But, overall, vehicle and air access are unrestricted. Airports offering national and international connections are found in Portland, in the south, and in Bangor, the state's second largest city. Many smaller airports suitable for use by private aircraft operate in various other cities and towns.

Most fishermen visiting Maine, however, do so by vehicle, and the state has a modern, well-maintained highway system. Coming from the south, the Maine Turnpike begins at Kittery and travels more than 100 miles north to Augusta, at which point Interstate 95 takes over — from Augusta north the highway is toll-free.

U.S. Route 1 also enters at Kittery, but travels along the coast all the way to Calais. It then travels northward to join Interstate 95 at Houlton; U.S. Route 1 ends at the town of Fort Kent in northern Aroostook County.

Other major routes within the state include Route 201, which travels from Interstate 95 at Fairfield northwestward through Jackman to the Canadian border; Route 2, which enters from New Hampshire at Bethel and ends at Bangor; and Route 302, which starts at Portland, travels northwestward to Sebago Lake, and exits into New Hampshire at Fryeburg. Other federal, state, and county highways crisscross the state. So access to just about any popular or worthwhile fishing area is fast, easy, and other than the Maine Turnpike, free.

Traveling in the remote areas, however, is quite different. Many of the roads in this vast country are ill-kept and constructed of gravel — springtime travel can be questionable. While the major woods hauling roads are maintained and upgraded annually, fishermen visiting these areas should understand the conditions and respect the fact that these roads — to some of Maine's better fishing grounds — are not intended for casual traffic.

A four-wheel drive vehicle is generally best. Standard pick-ups will get through to many places, but there are some areas where they will not. Automobiles and vans may be used on roads such as the Millinocket/Greenville Road and the access road into the Allagash from the West Branch — but speed should be restricted to 15 m.p.h. and caution should be used at all times.

As a rule, the roads needed to reach the better fishing spots are passable by the time fishing reaches its peak in late May or early June. Keep in mind, however, that late snows and heavy spring rains can make traveling in this region extremely hazardous. Tools and reasonable spare parts should be carried at all times.

Maine has been traditionally recognized as a trout and salmon fisherman's mecca. Sport fishing is extremely popular and, although the state is rapidly changing, fishing for these two species can still be considered among the best in the East. Native brook trout are found in lakes, ponds, rivers, streams, and brooks throughout the state, and a heavy brook trout stocking program is maintained where native strains have dwindled. Landlocked salmon are found in several hundred waters from York County north to Aroostook County — this aerobatic adversary is also highly prized. Brown trout are stocked in a number of rivers, streams, lakes, and ponds. And while rainbow trout are no longer managed in the state, remnant populations are still present, particularly in the upper Kennebec River. It is not difficult to see, therefore, that Maine does indeed have a great deal to offer the fisherman — this is the primary reason why the Pine Tree State continues to be one of the top fishing retreats in the country.

Maine has always been known primarily for its lakes and ponds. Few rivers and streams have, in the past, received the fishing attention or fame of Sebago Lake or Moosehead Lake, for instance, since it was once commonly thought that the biggest lakes supported the biggest fish, and thus the best fishing. Over the past few decades, however, this has gradually changed. The West Branch became renowned as a landlocked salmon river, the Kennebago was (and still is) considered one of the best native trout, and fall-run salmon, habitats. Fishermen suddenly discovered the great potential and challenge that Maine rivers and streams had to offer. And the interest in this type of habitat has been on the increase ever since. Today, Maine is recognized as having many highly productive and challenging trout and salmon rivers and streams. It is questionable whether rivers and streams will ever reach the popularity of lakes and ponds with Maine fishermen, but one thing is certain — the interest is there, and growing.

Maine streams and rivers are a diversified lot, changing with the terrain in various sections of the state. In the southern, central, and coastal sections, they are mostly fast-running, broken by an occasional rapid or riffle area flowing over a gravelly and rock-strewn bottom. Even in this day and age, the majority of them are clean, and concern by sportsmen and the general public about pollution and about dams without fishways or with barriers blocking fish passage has resulted in less fortunate waterways being restored. Waters where fish were not present at all two decades ago now (for the most part) offer fisheries, and the situation is gradually improving.

In the remaining regions of the state (the western mountains and northern "wilderness"), the majority of waterways remain as they were a century ago. Evidence of man *is* present, of course, and increasing annually. But the rivers and streams in these sections remain amazingly clean, most of them supporting good to excellent populations of trout and/or salmon.

In the high hills or mountains, a river or stream is characteristically fast-flowing, with a rocky or pebbly bottom, widening and slowing as it reaches the valleys and lowlands. Rapids and riffle stretches are common, particularly in the higher elevations, and each seems to have its share of deep pools, undercut banks, and typical trout and salmon holding areas. They are extremely challenging to fish productively, due to water clarity, water flow, and temperature. But acceptable fish *are* available.

No matter where you go in Maine, however, you will soon discover one important factor governing your success — Maine rivers and streams are typically not over-abundant with insect life. May flies and various species of caddis fly and stone fly, along with other important insect and terrestrial life, are present and do appear to aid the fly fisherman, but generally only for short, often sporadic periods throughout the open season.

In the south, central, and coastal regions, for example, May flies, caddis flies, and stone flies will start to appear (depending upon weather and water conditions) sometime in early to mid-May. Prominent hatches occur in June and early July also, with occasional, short hatches thereafter throughout the summer.

In the western hill country and northern remote areas, June is again the principal month, with hatches continuing into July. August can present some nice, highly productive emerges, particularly of caddis flies and stone flies. The May fly is active as well. But strong, consistent insect hatches are rare in Maine; it is the short, sporadic hatches, occurring for brief periods when conditions are perfect, upon which the resident and visiting fisherman must rely.

Maine trout and salmon are not overly selective when it comes to floating imitations. They cannot be considered *easy* to catch; the challenge is always present. But neither can it be said that stream and river fishing in Maine is overly difficult.

Matching the hatch is something few fly fishermen can do precisely, but this ability is really not required to find action on the majority of Maine streams. An imitation that matches the natural in color and size is usually all that is necessary, and many times, if proper presentation and drift are achieved, fish appear to hit just about any similar pattern during the height of a hatch. If a fisherman is able to detect what natural is appearing, and can match it from his selection of flies, that's fine. But, generally, an exact match is not required.

Small wet flies, bucktails, streamers, and nymphs are popular on Maine trout and salmon streams, and they take their share of fish annually. In the spring, especially when water levels are high, streamers and bucktails which imitate baitfish are best; wet flies and nymphs are most productive when a hatch is not in progress during the remainder of the season. A well-equipped fisherman visiting Maine should have a good selection of flies of various styles: streamers, bucktails, wet flies, nymphs, and dry flies. It is not necessarily a requirement to have a great many flies, but each style or pattern should be represented.

Below is a well-balanced selection of flies for Maine rivers and streams:

DRY FLIES

Adams, 12-14
Hendrickson, 12-14
March Brown, 12-14
Light Cahill, 12-14
Gray Fox, 12-16
Red Quill, 12-16
Quill Gordon, 12-16
Mosquito, 12-14
Gold-Ribbed Hare's Ear, 10-14
Henryville Special

WET FLIES

Quill Gordon, 12-14
March Brown, 10-12-14
Light Cahill, 12-14
Gold-Ribbed Hare's Ear, 12-14
Hendrickson, 12-14

NYMPHS

Atherton Light
Atherton Dark
March Brown
Hendrickson
Gray Nymph
Muskrat Nymph
Otter Nymph
Light Cahill
Iron Blue

STREAMERS AND BUCKTAIL

Gray Ghost, 6-10
Black Ghost, 6-10
Black Nose Dace, 6-10
Marabou (Yellow and White), 6-10
Mickey Finn, 6-10
Supervisor, 6-10
Tri-Color, 6-10
Muddler, 6-10
Hornburg, 6-10

Maine has a relatively short open water fishing season when compared to the rest of New England. This is more a matter of tradition than biology and there are few reasons (other than political) why the fishing seasons could not remain open longer, with proper regulation.

For the past number of years the open seasons have been as follows:

BROOKS AND STREAMS—April 1 - August 15 (In Aroostook County, May 1 - September 15; in Cumberland and York counties, April 1 - September 15.)

RIVERS—April 1 - September 15. (In Aroostook County, May 1 - September 15; some rivers remain open longer — check updated fishing regulations under specific river of interest for dates.)

The daily bag and possession limits and length limits on trout and salmon are apt to change from time to time. Fishermen should be sure to check the most up-to-date regulations for information.

Anyone fishing the inland waters of Maine is required to possess a valid fishing license, except non-residents under the age of 12 and residents under the age of 16. In 1981, the fishing license fees were listed as follows:

RESIDENT		NON-RESIDENT	
16 years and older	$10.00	Seasonal, age 16 and over	$31.00
Combination (hunting/-		Combination (fishing and	
fishing	17.00	big game hunting)	88.00
3-day	10.00	Age 12-15, inclusive	4.50
		15-day	21.00
		7-day	18.00
		3-day	10.00
		Alien, seasonal	51.00
		Alien, combination fishing	
		and big game hunting	141.00

Additional information on seasons and limits, and all non-resident licenses, may be obtained by writing the Maine Department of Inland Fisheries and Wildlife, 284 State Street, Station #41, Augusta, ME 04333. Non-resident fishing licenses may also be purchased at many sporting goods and tackle shops throughout the state and in other states in the Northeast.

Other helpful information sources include: Maine Publicity Bureau, 97 Winthrop Street, Hallowell, ME 04347 (Ask for their free publication, "Maine Guide To Fishing" which includes 44 pages of sporting camp, lodge and campground listings); Baxter State Park Authority Reservation Clerk, P.O. Box 540, Millinocket, Maine 04462; and The North Maine Woods, Sheridan Road, P.O. Box 382, Ashland, Maine 04732 (Ask for their kit and map on more than 2.5 million acres of timberlands in Aroostook, Piscataquis, and Penobscot counties).

NEW HAMPSHIRE

Wedged between Maine on the east and Vermont on the west, the State of New Hampshire consists of less than 9,500 square miles. But most of that territory is extremely scenic. For the most part the southern counties and the central region around Lake Winnipesaukee are the most densely populated. Major southern cities are Portsmouth, Manchester, Nashua, Keene, Rochester, Claremont, Laconia, and Concord (the capital), all located in the seven-county region south of the White Mountains. In the north, the largest city is Berlin, located on the Androscoggin River in Coos County.

The geography of New Hampshire is perhaps some of the most diverse in New England. The southern counties are primarily flat, with some low, rolling hills. Although the largest percentage of the state's population lives here, the area is still well-forested with abundant open space. The rivers and streams vary as well; some have freestone characteristics, while others are slow-moving, mixed with riffles or rapids.

The central region of New Hampshire is the home of the beautiful White Mountains. Elevations of several exceed 5,000 feet, with Mt. Washington topping the list at 6,288 feet. Much of the territory is remote, well-forested, and very rugged. The region is a popular four-season recreational and tourist attraction and because of this, fishermen will find well-maintained highways and roads and sufficient lodging and camping facilities.

Due to the mountainous terrain in this section, many of the rivers and streams offer challenges to trout fishermen. In the spring, water flow is fast from winter run-off. When levels recede, temperatures remain cool. This, coupled with the amazing clarity of the water and the flow rate, demands patience and tactful angling procedures. Some excellent trout — rainbows, brookies, and browns — are available, however, especially in the deeper pools and riffle sections.

Northern New Hampshire is a great deal like western and northern Maine. A land of rolling hills and evergreens, it is still relatively sparsely populated and offers the best "wilderness" or remote fishing in the state. The Androscoggin and Connecticut rivers flow through this magnificent country — good trout and/or salmon fishing is found in both. Smaller but equally challenging and productive rivers and streams are available, many offering native brook trout in their headwaters. And, like their southern New Hampshire counterparts, the majority are clean and provide varying challenges to the fly fisherman.

Generally, New Hampshire is not recognized as a great fishing state. Certain areas within its boundaries *are* extremely popular (the upper Connecticut River and Connecticut Lake area, the upper Androscoggin River, and certain other rivers and streams), but compared to several other states in the East, New Hampshire has just never received the angling attention and fame it rightly deserves. To put it plainly, some excellent trout and salmon fishing is waiting for the stream and river fisherman — right in the Granite State!

Native trout — brookies — are still found in nearly all counties of New Hampshire, particularly in the central and northern areas. What natural reproduction does not supply, a modern hatchery and stocking program does; eight state hatcheries and two federal hatcheries raise approximately 2.5 million trout and salmon annually and the majority are stocked prior to and during each open season. In the rivers and streams of New Hampshire, rainbow trout, brown trout, and landlocked salmon are available in addition to the brookies.

For the fly fisherman, rivers and streams in southern New Hampshire usually reach proper angling levels by early May. Depending upon winter conditions and spring rains this can vary by a week or so, but usually by the second week of May conditions are normalizing. From this time until the season's first insect hatches start to appear, small wet flies, streamers, bucktails, and nymphs are the best producers. Experience has shown me, however, that below-the-surface flies are generally more productive in the waters of southern and central New Hampshire throughout the fishing season.

The central section of the state, the region of the White Mountains, is not usually a welcome spot for fly fishermen until early June. Abundant run-off from the mountains is usually a problem in May, with rivers and streams reaching normal levels shortly after Memorial Day; spring rains can make this even later, however.

Even in early June, water temperatures are cold and insect life in the high country streams is limited. In the valleys and lower elevations, May flies, many caddis flies, and stone flies (this one sporadically) will begin appearing about the second week of June, the hatches stretching through mid-July. August can find many water levels low, particularly in the higher places, and subsequently poor fishing. But fish will still be found in some of the larger, deeper pools.

The northern counties of New Hampshire are much like western Maine. In the spring, when rivers and streams are high, fishing for trout and salmon with wet flies, streamers, and bucktails can be excellent; May usually starts the season off in this area. A month later, when water levels have receded, the majority of waters will experience good to excellent May fly and caddis fly hatches — floating imitations will then produce, particularly in the early morning and late afternoon and evening hours. This will continue through July, and often into early August. At this time, water temperatures are apt to get a bit too high for consistent surface action, although sporadic hatches will occur and small wet flies and nymphs can produce well.

September and October (some rivers stay open into October) are excellent times, too. If you enjoy fishing for landlocked salmon, this is without a doubt one of the most esthetically rewarding, and challenging, periods of the season on the upper Connecticut — the upper Androscoggin produces some big trout at this time, too. When a late season hatch is in progress, dry flies will do well; otherwise, nymphs and wet flies are best. Those patterns listed under "Maine" are all excellent.

The open fishing seasons and bag limits on trout and salmon are generous in New Hampshire. According to the latest "Summary of Freshwater Fishing Rules" (1981), the open seasons and limits are listed as follows:

TROUT (including brook, rainbow, brown, golden, and their hybrids) — The day before the fourth Saturday in April thru October 15. Seven fish limit. No minimum length.

SALMON — April 1 through September 30. Minimum length, 15 inches in most waters of the state. Two-fish daily limit.

Keep in mind that there are specific exceptions in each county. Many waters are open longer on certain species. And it is a good idea to check the most updated fishing regulations; seasons may vary from year to year.

Anyone fishing the inland waters of New Hampshire, resident or nonresident, over the age of 16 years must purchase an inland fishing license. In 1981, the license fees were as follows:

RESIDENT		NON-RESIDENT	
Hunting/Fishing		Fishing (Seasonal)	$21.00
Combination	$14.00	Fishing, 15-Day	16.00
Fishing Only	9.25	Fishing, 7-Day	11.00
Fishing (Under age 16)	Free	Fishing, 3-Day	7.75
		Fishing (Under age 16)	Free

Additional information, and non-resident fishing licenses, may be obtained by writing the New Hampshire Fish and Game Department, Concord, NH 03301. Non-resident fishing licenses may also be purchased at various sporting goods, general stores, and sporting camps throughout the state.

Other helpful information sources are: New Hampshire Division of Economic Development, Concord, NH 03301. Ask for New Hampshire Camping Guide, a folder listing over 100 camping areas for tents and/or camper trailers. For camping in state parks, write New Hampshire Division of Parks, Concord, NH 03301. For White Mountain National Forest information, write White Mountain National Forest, Laconia, NH 03246. For regional and local information contact: Dartmouth-

Lake Sunapee Region, Box 246, Lebanon, NH 03766; Lakes Region, Box 300, Wolfeboro, NH 03894; Merrimack Valley Region, 323 Franklin Street, Manchester, NH 03101; Monadnock Region, Box 269, Peterborough, NH 03458; Seacoast Region, Box 476, Exeter, NH 03833; White Mountain Region, Lancaster, NH 03584.

VERMONT

The state of Vermont is nationally known and recognized for many things — maple sugar, stone walls, country roads, rolling hills, and a simple way of life that is difficult (if not impossible) to find elsewhere in the country. To the fly fisherman, however, the Green Mountain State contains some of the best trout waters in the East — its fame as an angling state is worldwide.

Looking at Vermont, however, one might wonder where all the trout reside. There are few large lakes within the state and, compared to neighboring New Hampshire and New York, not many ponds. But a closer look will reveal miles upon hundreds of miles of brooks, streams, and rivers, the majority of them crystal clear and trout- and/or salmon-laden. While a certain number of lakes, reservoirs, and back-country ponds are available, it is the streams and rivers of Vermont which attract much of the fishing pressure each year. And Vermont is a stream fisherman's utopia, at least in the Northeast.

Vermont is the second largest state in New England, covering 9,609 square miles. It is wedge-shaped, separating New York state on the west from New Hampshire on the east. The state's northern boundary, which touches Quebec, is 130 miles long, while the southern line along the northern Massachusetts border stretches barely fifty miles. In a north south direction, however, a distance of about 230 miles, is some of the most scenic country in the Northeast.

Much of Vermont is still rural, as if it has forgotten time and progressed gradually in its own special way. Major cities are relatively few compared to the other New England states but towns, villages, and smaller cities (with populations of 1,000 to 10,000) are well distributed. Among the major population areas are Brattleboro, Bennington, Springfield, Rutland (on the edge of the Green Mountain National Forest),

White River Junction (on the Connecticut River), St. Johnsbury, Barre, Montpelier (the capital), Burlington (on beautiful Lake Champlain), and its neighboring cities of Winooski and Essex Junction.

For a state that is so rural, Vermont has a magnificent highway system. More than 13,650 miles of public highways crisscross from north to south and east to west — and vehicle access to just about every worthwhile trout stream is relatively quick and easy.

Major routes and interstates include Route 5, which travels north/south along the Connecticut River; Route 91, which stretches from central Massachusetts through Brattleboro, White River Junction, St. Johnsbury, and eventually to Canada; Route 89, which connects White River Junction with Barre, Montpelier, Burlington, and Canada; and Route 100, which travels the entire length of the state from North Troy, on the Quebec border, south through the Green Mountains to Stamford on the Massachusetts border.

An official Vermont highway map (a valuable aid for visiting anglers) is available free of charge by writing the Agency of Development and Community Affairs, Vermont Travel Division, 61 Elm Street, Montpelier, Vermont 05602.

The geography of Vermont is a pleasant mixture of rolling hills and mountains, valleys, and rich farmlands. The rivers and streams offer a flow of rapids, small falls, and slow stretches; each river or stream has its share of these characteristics, except for the high-country waters, which are mostly fast and freestone. Fishing these waterways is extremely exciting and very challenging, and populations of brook trout, brown trout, rainbow trout, and salmon are all available. Vermont maintains a large stocking program, although wild strains can be found throughout the state, particularly in the Green Mountain region and in the so-called "Northeast Kingdom".

Spring is apt to come late to Vermont, as it does to other northern New England areas. The high country supplies over-abundant snowmelt and spring run-off water, keeping many rivers and streams running high well into the season. In the midsection of the state it is not unusual for water levels to be overly high into mid-May or even slightly later.

This does not mean that trout fishing in Vermont is unproductive or not worthwhile before this time. On the contrary, southern county rivers such as the famed Battenkill and Hoosic can be extremely productive with nymphs and small wet flies in early May, and even dry flies as the season's first hatches appear. June is a banner month, as it is just about everywhere in New England, and sporadic success continues into early July. The warm summer months are generally slow, although limited action can be found in some of the deeper pools, riffle areas, and places where small tributaries enter the principal waterways. September and October can be very productive, especially with small wet flies and certain nymph patterns. October is my favorite angling month in Vermont. It is not only challenging to the fisherman in me, but the autumn-colored countryside and the nip in the air are esthetic boosts.

About a week or ten days following the start of angling success in Vermont, the rivers and streams in the state's central and northern sections are ready for the fly fisherman. This is only a general rule, and varies from year to year according to snowmelt and spring rains. But as a rule, water levels have receded and some of the season's principal hatches are starting to appear by the third week of May. Trout, and salmon in rivers where they are available, become active and fishing action starts to pick up.

Again, June is the primary month over much of Vermont. It is then (and in late May) that some of the legendary May flies appear; use the Hendrickson, Light Cahill, March Brown, and Grey Fox — trout fishing is at its peak at this time. In central and northern regions, May fly, caddis fly, and stone fly hatches will continue to emerge through July and sporadically through August and into early September; the Dun Variant and Blue Wing Olive are two big producers. During late September and October, dry flies are generally poor producers; small wet imitations, nymphs, and small streamers take over in most of Vermont's waters.

Traditionally, the open water fishing seasons in Vermont are generously long. In 1981, the "Digest of Fish and Game Laws" listed the open seasons as follows:

TROUT (including brook, brown and rainbow), April 11 through October 25.

SALMON — April 11 through October 25.

There are certain exceptions to these dates, but few effect rivers and streams. Also, these dates may vary from year to year. Fishermen should make it a point to check the most recent Vermont Fish and Game summary for accuracy at the time of their visit.

A Vermont fishing license is required to fish any lake, pond, reservoir, river, stream, or brook for any species. In 1981, the license fees were listed as follows:

RESIDENT		NON-RESIDENT	
Fishing	$ 5.00	Fishing (seasonal)	$15.00
Combination (hunting/-		14-Day	10.00
fishing	10.00	3-Day	6.00
		Combination (hunting/	
		fishing)	60.00

License fees may change slightly year to year. Fishermen should obtain additional regulations, season, bag limit, and license information by writing: Vermont Fish and Game Department, Agency of Environmental Conservation, Montpelier, Vermont 05602. Other helpful information sources include: "Vermont Guide To Fishing," available free of charge from the Vermont Fish and Game Department. This is a map of the entire state noting all waters where trout and salmon as well as other species may be found. Each river indicates the species it contains and quality of fishing by special symbols. Major highways and cities are also noted. This is a most helpful aid for fishermen visiting the state. For information on the Green Mountain National Forest, write Forest Supervisor, Green Mountain National Forest, Federal Bldg., 151 West Street, Rutland, Vermont 05701. Information is also available on the Lye Brook and Bristol Cliffs Wilderness areas at the same address. For camping information on Vermont's many state parks and forests, write the Agency of Environmental Conservation, Vermont Division of Forests, Parks and Recreation, Montpelier, Vermont 05602. A list of Vermont's 34 State Forests and 40 State Parks and other recreational areas is offered on the reverse side of the official state map. A list of more than 60 privately owned campgrounds located throughout the state is also provided. Finally, for general travel tips and visitor information write: Vermont State Chamber of Commerce, Box 37, Montpelier, Vermont 05602.

MASSACHUSETTS

I don't know of any state in New England that is more of an enigma than Massachusetts. Recognized as one of the most populated and highly industrialized states in the country, there still exists a great deal of woodland (65% of the land mass is still forested) in the Commonwealth.

While much of the eastern half and some of the central section of the state is clustered with large cities (the Boston metropolitan area, Lawrence, Lowell, Worcester, and Springfield, to name a few), there still exist wooded sections between these cities, and western Massachusetts is a mass of rolling hills and pleasant valleys.

Although a fisherman unfamiliar with this state might think otherwise, there are many exciting rivers and streams containing several varieties of trout in Massachusetts. In certain areas, native populations of squaretails still remain, but much of the fishing relies on a large stocking program. Nevertheless, during my several visits to the state I have always found challenging and magnificent fly fishing.

Getting to the better fishing spots is not a problem in the Bay State. Major interstate highways cross the state in east/west and north/south directions and vehicle travel is fast, easy, and convenient. The major highways and interstates travel from the major cities to some of the better trout waters in the state.

For the most part, the best trout fishing is in the central and western counties of the state. The Cape Cod region does have a number of fine waters, and there are limited possibilities in other eastern areas. The topnotch rivers and streams, however, are in the less populated sections. Travel time from Boston or other major New England cities is only a matter of a few hours. It takes me about four hours to reach the Deerfield River from my southern Maine home. From Boston, it can be reached in approximately two and one-half hours; from Hartford, Connecticut, in two hours and ten minutes and from Albany, New York in three and one-half hours. Other major rivers can be reached in similarly short travel times.

Massachusetts is a central New England state, and because of this, trout fishing starts a little earlier than in Maine, New Hampshire, and Vermont. Waters on most central Massachusetts rivers are apt to be at fishable levels by late April or early May. By the second week of May, things are really rolling, with ideal water temperatures and the appearance of major hatches; use the Black Quill along with the Quill Gordon anytime after the third week of April, followed by the Dark Brown Spinner and Hendrickson or Red Quill in late April or sometime in May.

June is, again, the prime month during a normal year. Insect hatches reach their peak at this time and fishing is excellent just about everywhere. May fly species which appear at this time can be matched with flies like the March Brown (the first week of June, as a rule), the Grey Fox, the Light Cahill, the Blue-Winged Olive and the Dun Variant.

July can be a slow period, except on rivers controlled by dams (such as the Swift River coming out of the southern end of the Quabbin Reservoir). Water levels fluctuate daily and temperatures remain cool throughout the season — thus, fishing is productive at specific times. For the remainder of the season, small wet flies, nymphs, and streamers are best.

The western rivers and streams of Massachusetts become fishably active generally about ten days to two weeks following the central waterways. This varies from year to year depending upon winter run-off and spring rains, but usually by mid-May all elements are working together and fishing starts to pick up.

The insect hatches mentioned for the central waters become visibly active about two weeks later in the Berkshire region. For example, the Black Quill fly works well on the Deerfield or Westfield Rivers sometime around April 30, the Dark Brown Spinner about May 15, etc. Fishermen visiting this section of the state should plan accordingly (see Chapter Two for more insect hatch emergence information).

June is an excellent month in the Berkshires and other western and highcountry areas. Dry flies are best during a hatch or when surface feeding is evident, with small wet flies and small nymphs doing well at other times. July is questionable, although some good trout are possible. September and October are fine times with below-the-surface offerings.

The open water fishing seasons in Massachusetts are adequately long, similar to those in New Hampshire and Vermont. In 1981 the open season on rivers and streams was listed as follows:

RIVERS AND STREAMS: April 18 through October 18.

There are exceptions to these dates; fishermen should check the latest "Massachusetts Abstracts of the Fish and Wildlife Laws" for additional details. Fees are as follows:

RESIDENT		NON-RESIDENT & NON-RESIDENT ALIENS	
Seasonal	$11.25	Fishing seasonal	$17.25
Minors between the ages of 15 and 17	6.25	7-day	11.25
Resident Aliens	14.25		

Additional license, regulation and bag limit information, along with all non-resident fishing licenses, may be obtained by writing Massachusetts Division of Fisheries and Wildlife, I.&E. Division, Rt. 135, Westboro,

MA 01581. Non-resident fishing licenses may also be purchased at numerous sporting goods and tackle shops throughout the state.

A helpful information source is: Massachusetts Division of Forests and Parks, 100 Cambridge Street, Boston, MA 02202.

Chapter 2

The Hatches and Imitations

There are not too many places I'd rather be than on a trout stream during a dun emergence. One other place I *can* readily think of, however, is on a trout stream during a spinner flight or fall; both are most intriguing, interesting, and challenging periods to be astream. And, fortunately, the rivers and streams of northern New England have much to offer in these areas.

Not every stream in our section of the country is blessed with an overabundance of insect life, however. Each appears to have at least a minimal supply of May fly, caddis fly and stone fly species. But New England waters are generally less fortunate than those in other areas — Pennsylvania, for instance, or many of the western states. This baffles many fly fishing enthusiasts, for the majority of our trout and salmon streams appear clean and healthy. But what they lack is the proper acidity levels and other ingredients needed to sustain healthy insect populations. This does not mean, however, that New England rivers and streams are completely devoid of insect life.

Many of our hatches are legendary; Hendricksons, Quill Gordons, Blue-Wing Olives, and March Browns, for example. Yet the average fly fisherman looking for brook trout action on Maine's Kennebago River or brown trout on Vermont's Battenkill would not recognize a *Stenonema vicarium* (March Brown) if they saw one. It took me years to learn to recognize some of the more important, principal Northeast naturals, and I'm still learning.

It has always been my belief that too much emphasis has been placed on "matching the hatch." While it is definitely a great help to know which species of May fly is hatching while astream and then be able to match it with an imitation, such knowledge takes years to acquire. Many frustrating and unproductive hours can pass before the average fly fisherman reaches that point. Knowing whether to fish a dun or a spinner imitation is also helpful — but only experience, and time, will tell you this.

By observing and matching *two* basic characteristics of whatever natural happens to be appearing over the water, some measure of success can be gained while learning. Those two characteristics are *color* and *size*.

Basically, the three most important species to fly fishermen are the May fly (order *Ephemeroptera*), the caddis fly (order *Trichoptera*) and the stone fly (order *Plecoptera*). The greatest concentrations of May flies are found in slow- to medium-flowing rivers and streams; peak activity periods are during the weeks of spring and early summer, although some species continue to emerge until fall.

The natural May fly, in adult form, varies in size and color — the imitations we carry should do the same. As a rule, dry flies designed to resemble May fly species are tied on hook sizes ranging from #6 to #20. Smaller hooks (down to #24) are sometimes used; the most popular, however, are those from #10 through #16.

Colors of the May fly species vary as much as sizes, involving virtually every color of the rainbow. Some of the more prominent shades are brown, black, white, cream, dark blue, pale blue, bluish gray, gray, ginger, olive, and tan. If at all possible, floating imitations should be carried in these colors and in sizes from #10 to #16, maybe even a bit smaller.

Like the May fly, the caddis fly varies a great deal in size and coloration. The best floating imitations are those from #8 or #10 down to #16, although smaller hook sizes can produce well under certain circumstances. The best caddis fly hatches take place following those of the May fly from early summer (mid-June) through fall, although sporadic appearances are found earlier; the caddis fly prefers medium- to fast-flowing water.

Adult caddis imitations have become extremely popular in recent years for one good reason: they hook trout and salmon. On many streams in New England, the caddis fly is becoming more dominant as the May fly falls victim to warmer water temperatures or pollution and stream alteration in rural areas. And while the May fly continues to be the most single important insect to the fly fisherman, the caddis is gaining ground in many areas.

Personally, I like using adult caddis imitations. Well dressed, they float well and can be easily and properly "skittered" over the surface to imitate the performance of the natural. My fly box usually contains a wide assortment of down-wing patterns in gray, brownish gray, brown, black, light yellow, olive, dark green, cream, brownish tan, tan, and reddish brown. Among my favorite caddis imitations are the Henryville Special, the Hairwing Caddis in a variety of color combinations, and the Woodchuck Caddis, all in various hook sizes.

Like the May fly and caddis fly, the adult stone flies are best imitated by flies that reproduce the color and size of the natural. As a rule, adult members of the order *Plecoptera* are large, although small members of the order are sometimes seen streamside. The fly fisherman should be concerned with imitations in sizes ranging from #6 down to about #14 or #16 for this section of the country. Those flies in colors or pale yellow, brown, green, black, yellow, and light orange (or a combination of these shades) are best. Some prime examples include Bird's Stonefly and the Sofa Pillow.

Selecting a diverse dry fly collection for a specific section of the country is always a challenge. To aid those just beginning, the following list of dry fly patterns is suggested for fishing New England trout and salmon streams. Keep in mind, however, that this is a basic list covering the most important or prominent naturals. At times, other lesser known flies or "regional favorites" must be considered. Each pattern should be carried in various sizes — and remember to match the natural's basic color and size.

SUGGESTED DRY FLY PATTERNS FOR FISHING NEW ENGLAND TROUT AND SALMON STREAMS

CADDIS FLY IMITATIONS	STONE FLY IMITATIONS
Bucktail Caddis	Bird's Stonefly
Hairwing Caddis	Sofa Pillow
Woodchuck Caddis	Improved Bird's
Soloman's Hairwing	Stonefly
Vermont Caddis	

MAY FLY IMITATIONS

Adams	Black Gnat
Quill Gordon	Cream Variant
Hendrickson	Grey Fox
Light Cahill	Green Drake
Mosquito	March Brown
Blue Wing Olive	Red Quill

Being on a trout stream during the height of a hatch is truly one of the most exciting experiences a fly fisherman will ever have. However, most fishermen do not know exactly when a certain May fly or caddis fly species is apt to emerge. There are few published works which offer such information, so the fisherman is left to speculate when the March Brown might appear on the Battenkill, or when the Hendrickson might create action on the upper Connecticut.

During my travels I have tried to keep records that accurately indicate when some of the more renowned and important insect hatches appear on northern New England waters. I would like to offer that data now, with the understanding of the reader that the hatch dates mentioned will vary from year to year according to water and environmental conditions. They are, however, as accurate as possible.

It should also be understood that most insect species hatch at various times in different regions of each state. In Maine, for example, the Blue-Wing Olive appears on southern and some central waters starting about June 20. But northern and western mountain streams do not see the Blue-Wing Olive until approximately a week to ten days later, given normal water and weather conditions. This is true for much of northern New England, and I have therefore offered *two* hatching dates under each state. Keep in mind all hatching dates are *approximate.*

MAINE

INSECT IMITATION	HATCHING DATE SOUTHERN	HATCHING DATE NORTHERN	BEST TIME TO FISH
Black Quill	May 5	May 13	early afternoon to dusk
Quill Gordon	May 2	May 11	noon to 3 p.m.
Iron Blue Dun	May 8	May 16-20	4:30 p.m. to dusk
Grey Drake	May 21	May 28 - June 1	4:00 p.m. to dusk
Brown Stonefly	May 20-23	June 3	2 p.m. to 4 p.m.

Pale Evening Dun	June 19	June 25	late evening
March Brown	May 22	May 29	noon to 3 p.m.
Grey Fox	May 26	May 30	noon to 3 p.m.
Light Cahill	June 1	June 8	late evening
Hendrickson	June 20	June 25	2 p.m. to 5 p.m.
Dun Variant	July 10	July 16-20	late evening to dusk
Blue-Wing Olive	July 20	July 25	dusk

Caddis hatches in southern Maine start to appear in late April, with May and June being top months; sporadic hatches are seen throughout the season. In the north, caddis become important starting in mid-May.

NEW HAMPSHIRE

(Keep in mind that central and northern New Hampshire is extremely mountainous; insect hatches are subject to severe spring run-off and cold water conditions; hatches may appear up to 15 days later than those in the south.)

INSECT IMITATION	HATCHING DATE SOUTHERN	HATCHING DATE NORTHERN	BEST TIME TO FISH
Quill Gordon	April 28	May 10	noon to 2:30 p.m.
Hendrickson	May 7	May 20	2 p.m. to 4 p.m.
Iron Blue Dun	May 8	May 20-21	late afternoon to early evening
Pale Evening Dun	May 28	June 10-12	evening
March Brown	May 25	June 10	late afternoon to late evening
Light Cahill	June 1	June 12-15	late afternoon to late evening
Blue-Wing Olive	June 20	July 5	noon to evening

Most caddis hatches in southern New Hampshire start in late May and appear sporadically throughout much of the season. In northern areas, mid-June through July is excellent, with sporadic hatches seen to the end of the trout season.

VERMONT

INSECT IMITATION	HATCHING DATE SOUTHERN	HATCHING DATE NORTHERN	BEST TIME TO FISH
Hendrickson	May 17	May 21	2:30 to 4:00 p.m.
March Brown	May 21	May 24	noontime to about 4:00 p.m.
Light Cahill	May 25	May 26	early evening to dusk
Grey Fox	May 25	May 26	noontime to about 4:00 p.m.
Dun Variant	July 10	July 10	early evening
Blue-Wing Olive	July 25	July 25	early to late evening

MASSACHUSETTS

INSECT IMITATION	HATCHING DATE EASTERN	HATCHING DATE WESTERN	BEST TIME TO FISH
Black Quill	April 16	April 28	mid to late afternoon
Quill Gordon	April 16-24	May 3	noontime to 3 p.m.
Hendrickson	May 9	May 22	2:00 p.m. - dusk
March Brown	May 30	June 10	11:00 a.m. to late afternoon, early evening
Light Cahill	June 8	June 18	late afternoon to dusk
Grey Fox	June 8	June 18	late afternoon to early evening
Blue-Wing Olive	June 15	June 20	early afternoon to mid-evening

On Massachusetts' two principal trout streams, the Deerfield and Swift rivers, good May fly and caddis fly hatches will be available throughout much of the season, but only sporadically after the peak activity periods.

A final note concerning the hatching data just offered: although many of the May fly species start to appear on or about the dates mentioned, keep in mind that many have lengthy emergence duration periods, lasting from several weeks to four months. While other species may be primarily active for shorter periods, from 10 to 20 days, sporadic activity is common on just about every northern New England trout stream.

Not every trout or salmon caught is taken on a dry fly. And although I'd rather cast a #14 March Brown or Hendrickson to a rising brown, brookie, rainbow, or salmon, I have to admit that more fish are taken below the surface with wet flies, streamers, and nymphs than with hackled imitations.

There was a time when I didn't enjoy fishing with below-the-surface flies. I was a dry fly "purist," utilizing wet counterparts only when fishing for spring salmon or during specific times of the season when I absolutely knew that dry offerings were useless, or nearly so.

Now, however, I rather enjoy wet designs. I still prefer to challenge rising adversaries. But I no longer "refuse" to use wet flies, streamers, and bucktails — or nymphs, for that matter. I must say that presenting a #14 or 16 Hendrickson, or a small nymph, getting a proper drift, and anticipating the strike, are most challenging, exciting, and rewarding pastimes. Throughout the fishing season, the majority of my trout and salmon are taken on below-the-surface flies.

WET FLIES, STREAMERS, AND NYMPHS FOR LANDLOCKED SALMON

The landlocked salmon is a cherished adversary in many rivers and streams of northern New England — this fish is highly susceptible to streamers, bucktails, wet flies, and nymphs. While they will rise to a floating fly during periods of peak insect activity, the majority are taken with below-the-surface flies.

In Maine, the West Branch of the Penobscot, the Rapid, the Kennebago, Grand Lake Stream, and the Roach are among the top salmon rivers. In New Hampshire, salmon will be found in the upper Connecticut River, and the species will be found in various rivers of Vermont entering Lake Champlain during the spring and fall.

Starting in the spring, when the majority of rivers and streams in northern New England are high and cold with run-off water, the best flies for landlocked salmon are the streamer and bucktail. Patterns tied to imitate important forage fish such as the smelt, shiner, and dace are excellent, as are "attractor" designs. At this time, such flies as the Grey Ghost, Black Ghost, Nine-Three, Supervisor, Mickey Finn, the White and Yellow Marabou, Barnes Special, and Red and White should be considered.

Hook sizes from #4 through #10, attached to a leader tapering down to a 2½- to 4-pound test tippet and sinking or sinking tip line are most popular. Streamers and bucktails are best fished deep in pools or on the edge or tail end of a riffle area, and should be worked antagonizingly or in a manner to resemble the bait fish being imitated.

As water levels recede and start to warm, landlocked salmon will accept many of the popular trout wet flies and nymphs. Once the rivers and streams reach normal flow levels, salmon like to hold in areas with high oxygen content and slightly cooler temperatures. This means the pools and riffles again, where sinking lines or sinking tip lines must be employed. When using nymphs, however, a floating line may be used, although on some of the larger salmon rivers I've often found that a sinking tip line gets the offering down more quickly to areas where salmon are apt to be lying.

For a list of good landlocked salmon wet flies and nymphs, see the section entitled "WET FLIES, STREAMERS, AND NYMPHS FOR TROUT" later in this chapter.

THE FALL RUN LANDLOCKED SALMON

In the fall, sometime between late August and mid-September, several of northern New England's rivers and streams experience one of the most unique natural phenomenons anywhere — the fall run. Basically, the fall run is the movement or migration of mature landlocked salmon upstream into major tributaries of large lakes in preparation to spawn; examples of such rivers are the Crooked, which enters Maine's Sebago Lake; the Kennebago, which enters Mooselookmeguntic Lake (also in Maine); and the Connecticut River, which drains the Connecticut Lakes and Lake Francis in northern New Hampshire.

While the fall run is characterized as a "migration" of salmon, not all rivers with populations of this species enter a larger body of water, although most do. But a general *characteristic* change is evident in land-locked salmon at this time, no matter where they are found.

Influenced by drastic changes in water levels, temperatures, and light conditions, the landlocks lose their territorial and cannibalistic instincts and strike a fly more from aggression or irritation than from the desire to feed. Because of this, fishing for the landlocked salmon during the fall run is considered one of the most demanding challenges in northern New England. A fly fisherman must be patient and present his fly properly time after time to an area where the fish will see it.

Fishing for autumn landlocks is unlike fishing for this species during any other period of the open season. In the early spring, we try to imitate important forage fish or match an emerging insect. But in the fall, we must attract the attention of the fish and irritate him enough to draw a strike. This means placing the offering within the immediate resting area of the fish and working it in an antagonizing way. Success is often judged by a fisherman's skill at casting, his patience, and his ability to read a pool or riffle area to determine where a salmon might be lying.

The movements of migrating salmon are influenced by light. Bright, clear days will often find them holding in secluded pockets, undercut banks, and deep pools. Primary movement is restricted to the hours of dusk and early morning, before the sun has a chance to hit the water.

Ideally, the best time to fish for fall salmon is on cloudy, overcast days, or even when it's raining or drizzling. Salmon are most active when water levels are rising or turbid, and on overcast days, light is restricted. Again, however, I prefer to fish early in the morning on such days, from dawn to about 10 a.m. and again from about 4 p.m. to dusk or shortly after; salmon are most active at this time. But, on adverse weather days, I would not hesitate to cast a line at any time. On clear days, the early morning-late afternoon to dusk rule prevails.

Small wet flies and nymphs are the best offerings for fall salmon. Occasionally, fishermen will witness fish rising, or "porpoising", but this does not necessarily mean they are actively feeding. While I have taken salmon on dry flies during the migration, I have found that below-the-surface flies are more productive at this time.

Suggested "fall run" landlocked salmon flies:

WET FLIES		NYMPHS	
Name	Size	Name	Size
Coachman	8-14	Hare's Ear Nymph	6-14
Hare's Ear	8-14	Otter Nymph	6-14
Olive Heron	8-10	Tellico	8-14
Leadwing Coachman	8-12	Zug Bug	8-14
Grey Hackle	8-14	Atherton Dark	10-14
Picket Pin	8-14	Atherton Light	10-14
Black Woolly Worm	6-12	Martinez	10-14

WET FLIES, STREAMERS
AND NYMPHS FOR TROUT

The fish species that New England fishermen call "trout" — the brown (a member of the salmonid family), the brookie (a char), and the rainbow (a true trout) — spend relatively little time throughout the fishing season feeding on the surface of a stream or river. As a matter of fact, trout actually feed on mature May flies, caddis flies, stone flies, and other adult insect life only about ten percent of the time that our waters are free of ice — this obviously makes wet flies, streamers, and nymphs extremely important baits.

Basically, wet flies and streamers can entice trout into striking whenever surface action is not evident, as in the early spring when trout are apt to be feeding on small forage fish and tiny insect larvae moving about the bottom or being forced along with the current. Wet flies are the oldest form of artificial flies and are tied generally to imitate immature insects that live in an aquatic environment. Fished properly, they are extremely productive and are useful throughout the open water fishing season. Streamers and bucktails, as I have previously stated, are often designed to imitate important forage fish; they work equally as well on trout or salmon.

Selecting an adequate wet fly and streamer selection for the trout species inhabiting New England rivers and streams is not a difficult job. Many of the popular and more productive dry designs have a wet counterpart, and fishermen frequently, and wisely, carry wet flies that have the same names as dry flies. For example, one of my favorite floating imitations is the March Brown, and one of my favorite wet designs is the March Brown tied in the wet fashion.

A suggested list of wet flies for this region follows:

Blue Dun, size 8-14
Dark Cahill, size 10-16
Light Cahill, size 10-16
Quill Gordon, size 12-18
Hare's Ear, size 12-16

Light Hendrickson, size 12-16
Dark Hendrickson, size 12-16
Female Beaverkill, size 12-16
Iron Blue Dun, size 12-16
March Brown, size 12-16

Here are some other imitative and non-imitative designs that are equally as productive at times, and which should be considered:

Professor, size 8-14

Grey Hackle, size 8-16

Leadwing Coachman, size 10-16

Parmachene Belle, size 8-14

Picket Pin, size 8-14

Woolly Worm, size 6-12

Yellow Sally, size 12-14

Black Gnat, size 10-14

Scarlet Ibis, size 12-14

Ginger Quill, size 12-14

It isn't necessary, of course, to carry every fly mentioned in this list. But wet flies are without question very effective tools with which to fool trout, and one never knows which will be most productive. So it helps to have a good selection from which to choose.

Streamer flies are also productive for trout fishing in rivers and streams. The flies suggested earlier in this chapter for salmon will often attract the attention of a brown, rainbow, or squaretail but I would also recommend the following:

Muddler, size 8-12

Hornburg, size 6-10

Black Nose Dace, size 6-10

Little Brook Trout, size 6-10

Light Edson Tiger, size 6-10

Dark Edson Tiger, size 6-10

Warden's Worry, size 8-10

Nymphs are probably the least used artificial flies, particularly among novice fly fishermen. This is true not because the nymph is less productive than other wet forms or than dry flies, but rather because proper utilization of the nymph imitation demands understanding of natural insects in their nymph forms, the reactions of trout to insects in this stage of the life cycle, and the ways to present and utilize them correctly. It takes considerable time to obtain the skill to use nymphs properly. The strike on a nymph is less dramatic than on a dry fly, one reason for the low popularity of nymph fishing.

Some of northern New England's finer trout and salmon streams offer excellent fishing opportunities to the fly fisherman willing to put nymphs to use. During the spring, before adult insects rise to the surface, a well delivered nymph imitation will produce excellent results. Nymphs are also some of the best flies throughout the season if surface action is not available.

I strongly suggest that the fly fisherman who has never taken the time to utilize nymphs give it a try. Not only will his knowledge of trout and salmon and their relations to insect life increase, but his success rate under more varied conditions will most likely increase, too. Nymphing is not easy to master, but it is a challenging, most rewarding, and productive way to fly fish.

The following list of nymphs is suggested for New England trout and salmon streams:

Hare's Ear Nymph, sizes 8-18
Otter Nymph, sizes 8-14
Atherton Dark, sizes 10-16
Green Drake (Ephemera)
   Nymph, sizes 6-10
Hendrickson (Ephemerella)
   Nymph, sizes 10-14
March Brown (Stenonema)
   Nymph, sizes 10-14
Black Nymph, sizes 8-14

Bird's Stonefly Nymph
   No. 2, sizes 6-10
Gray Midge Mymph, sizes 14-22
Muskrat Nymph, sizes 8-14
Gray Nymph, sizes 12-14
Quill Gordon Nymph,
   sizes 12-14
Light Cahill Nymph,
   sizes 12-14
Tellico, sizes 8-14
Zug Bug, sizes 8-14

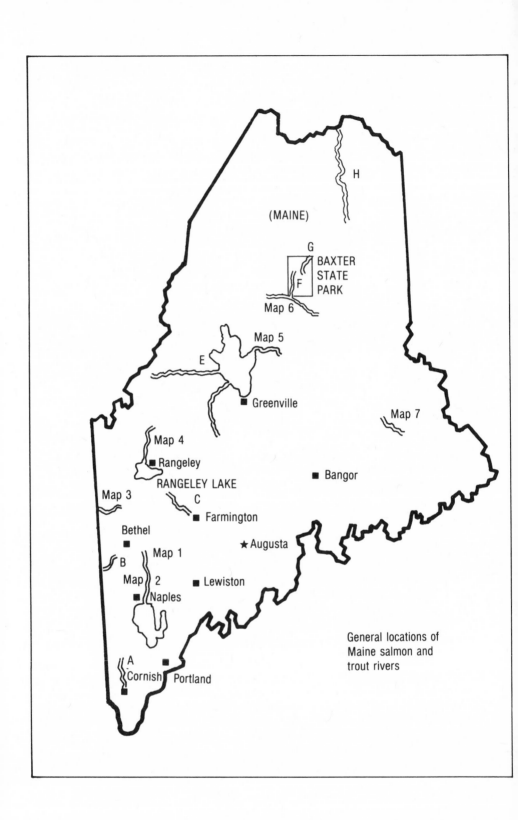

General locations of
Maine salmon and
trout rivers

Chapter 3
The Rivers of Maine

For the most part, those rivers and streams of Maine which contain trout and salmon will provide the fly fisherman with good to excellent sport throughout much of the open water fishing season. While mid-May through the end of June, and the month of September, are generally accepted as the two peak activity periods, action does continue on most watersheds into and through the hotter months of the summer.

The visiting fisherman should keep in mind, however, that water levels and temperatures *do* fluctuate as the season progresses. In the south, many of the rivers and streams may be considered "low" by mid-July (or slightly earlier), and consistent fishing tapers off. In the mountain regions of the west, run-off water is gone by late May, allowing rivers to flow at normal levels for a month or so before dropping; this is approximately what happens in the northern sections, too.

Generally speaking, rivers and streams in Maine flow in a north-to-south direction. In the extreme north, some waters break this pattern. While some flow parallel to highways or rural roads, resulting in relatively easy access, others require a general knowledge of the area and its access points. The maps included in each river section of this book provide some such information, but please understand that these maps are not meant to go into great detail, and some exploring may be required.

Certain rivers in Maine have limited access facilities; the fisherman should know the capabilities of his vehicle and be prepared for any emergency.

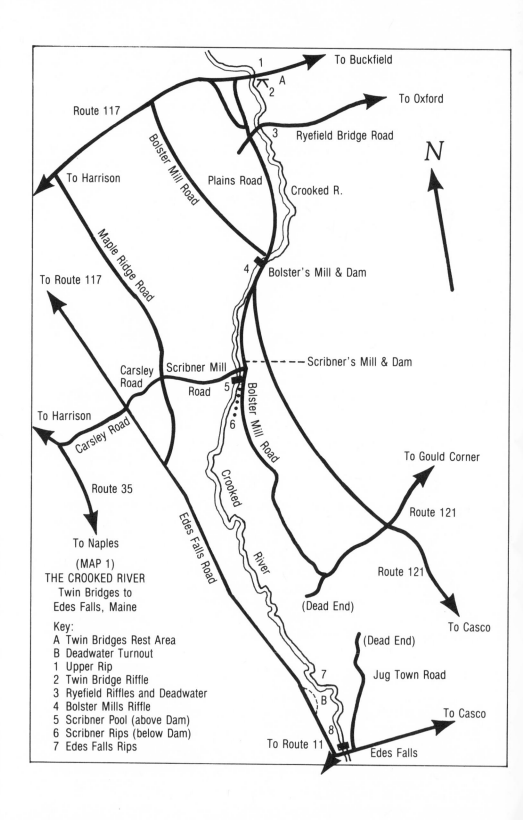

To Buckfield

To Oxford

N

Route 117

Bolster Mill Road

Ryefield Bridge Road

To Harrison

Plains Road

Crooked R.

Maple Ridge Road

Bolster's Mill & Dam

To Route 117

Scribner's Mill & Dam

Carsley Road

Scribner Mill Road

Bolster Mill Road

To Harrison

Carsley Road

To Gould Corner

Route 121

Route 35

Crooked River

Route 121

To Naples

Edes Falls Road

(Dead End)

(MAP 1)
THE CROOKED RIVER
Twin Bridges to
Edes Falls, Maine

(Dead End)

Jug Town Road

Key:
A Twin Bridges Rest Area
B Deadwater Turnout
1 Upper Rip
2 Twin Bridge Riffle
3 Ryefield Riffles and Deadwater
4 Bolster Mills Riffle
5 Scribner Pool (above Dam)
6 Scribner Rips (below Dam)
7 Edes Falls Rips

To Casco

To Route 11

Edes Falls

THE CROOKED RIVER

Twin Bridges to Edes Falls

GENERAL DESCRIPTION

The Crooked River starts its journey southward from Songo Pond in the town of Albany in Oxford County, approximately 15 miles southwest of Bethel. From its source to its confluence with the Songo River a mile north of Sebago Lake, a total distance of 42.5 miles is covered, the river flowing through or touching seven different towns.

Without question, the Crooked River is southern Maine's best land-locked salmon and native brook trout fishery. It serves as one of the major spawning and rearing tributaries for Sebago Lake, and each spring and fall large numbers of salmon are found moving upstream after smelt or on their own spawning run. While landlocked salmon between two and three pounds are average along most of the Crooked at various times of the season, examples weighing four and five pounds are taken, particularly in the fall.

The Crooked River also offers a limited brook trout fishery. The Maine Department of Inland Fisheries and Wildlife does not stock trout in this river — thus all trout caught are native. Populations can be found along the Crooked's entire length. But the best trout section is from Scribner's Mill upstream past Twin Bridges to the river's source and off major tributaries in the spring. The river is swift in many areas, providing excellent habitat throughout the year.

Characteristically, the Crooked River could be considered a rapid flowing watershed. Within its 42.5-mile length, it drops in elevation a total of 388 feet, thus offering the fly fisherman a mixture of rapids, riffles, deep pools, and slow stretches. The rapid and riffle areas are strong and swift in the spring, but are a pleasant challenge throughout the season, except during the extreme warm weeks of summer. It is in these faster stretches where some of the best fishing is found, and most of them are easily accessible, either by vehicle or by a short walk.

There are some real advantages to fishing the Crooked River. Overall, it is not a large flowage (ranging between 25 and 40 feet in width) — wading is fairly easy. Because of its width and flow at normal levels, properly casting and delivering a fly is not difficult — and besides, it is an esthetically rewarding river to explore and fish.

From Twin Bridges downstream to Edes Falls in Naples, the river flows through a wooded valley, only occasionally crossing roads or coming within sight of houses. When on the river in this section, the fisherman will often be quite alone, although some of the more popular riffles and pools will be shared at peak periods. However, there is enough river to accommodate the pressure — and I've found some of my favorite "fishing holes" by exploring when major spots were busy: fishermen unfamiliar with the river should do the same. Some excellent pools, riffles, and pocket water can be found "off the beaten path", but still near access points marked on the map. Quite often, these prove more productive than the easily reached or more popular counterparts.

BEST PLACES TO FISH

Finding productive fishing areas on the Crooked is not difficult. From Twin Bridges to Edes Falls, several roads either cross the river or offer access via a short hike. A few of these roads are dirt (passable by most automobiles), while the majority are paved.

Route 17 crosses the Crooked River in the town of Harrison. After crossing the bridge heading east, there is a nice picnic area on the right. Here, the river is fairly swift, providing magnificent riffles both above and below the bridge, broken by occasional pools. This is a productive stretch for salmon in the fall, once they have moved up from sections downstream. By parking here and walking either up or downstream, additional pools and minor riffles can be reached.

On the Harrison side of the river (the west bank looking downstream) the Plains Road travels south, eventually entering the small hamlet of Bolster's Mills. Approximately three miles from Route 17, the Ryefield Bridge Road heads east, crossing the river approximately one-half mile away. The river is slower in this section, but salmon are caught here, particularly in middle or late September after a heavy rain, when salmon are moving up river.

The Plains Road continues on to Bolster's Mills. Below the dam, the river offers a mass of riffles and rapids, where fall-fun salmon congregate before making a final push into the dam; this area can offer excellent fishing.

Crossing the river at Bolster's, the fisherman can turn south and follow the Bolster's Mills Road to the Scribner's Mills Road, which comes in on the right about three miles downstream. This dirt road goes to Scribner's Mills.

On the upstream side of the dam, there is a magnificent long pool offering some excellent fishing opportunities, as salmon hold here in the fall after moving over the dam. There are some good areas upstream, but they have no access points other than bushwhacking along the river's edge.

On the east bank of the river looking downstream from the bridge at Scribner's, however, a logging road has been cut which parallels the river for some distance. There are some rolling riffles and deep pools within sight of this road and they are worth spending some time on. The road enters a field which provides ample parking; the fisherman can work downstream and discover some magnificent water.

From the dam, the Scribner's Mills Road travels west, joining the Maple Ridge Road about a mile away. Turn right, then take an immediate left on the Carsley Road. Approximately one and a half miles west, the Edes Falls Road enters on the left; this partly paved, partly dirt road travels south along the river, although the river cannot be seen until just above Edes Falls.

Just above the falls, on the left side of the road going south, there is a turnout. This is a good spot to put in a canoe, and paddling upstream the fisherman will find some productive riffles and pools that receive little angling attention.

Good fishing can be found both above and below Edes Falls. The quiet water just above the dam is a popular resting spot for fish that have ascended the falls, and the pool at the bridge is a holding spot for fish before they battle the rapids. There is a stretch of quiet water downstream, which can also produce excellent results.

BEST TIMES TO FISH

Traditionally, the Crooked River is recognized as a "fall run" river. And, although salmon populations can be found in certain sections of the river throughout much of the season, fall is still the best time.

Salmon start to move gradually upstream from Sebago Lake sometime in late August. A heavy rain will induce movement, but fishing usually starts to pick up by the first week of September and peaks by the third week, with excellent opportunities continuing until the close of the season. Keep in mind, however, that a rise in water level is needed to pull salmon upstream, and low water levels can greatly reduce success.

BEST FLIES

Every fisherman who works a stream or casts a line for landlocked salmon has a special fly, or several favorite flies, that he knows will work. When fishing the Crooked for fall salmon, however, action has much to do with water levels.

After a heavy rain, for example, when water levels rise suddenly, small #6 or #8 casting streamers such as the Black Ghost, Grey Ghost, or Supervisor will take fish in the pools and on the edges of riffle areas. During other periods, small wet flies such as the Hare's Ear, Hendrickson, Cahill, or Coachman will work. So will nymphs; the Otter and Muskrat patterns are excellent, and the Hare's Ear is another good one.

I have often found, on any "fall run" salmon river, that the type of fly used is not as important as *how* it is used, where it is placed, and the level of the fisherman's patience. While it always helps to know what fly will draw the most attention, patient and proper placing and working of just about any below-the-surface fly is apt to produce action.

HOW TO REACH THE CROOKED RIVER
AT TWIN BRIDGES (DOWNSTREAM)

From Portland, take Route 302 north to Sebago Lake, passing through North Windham and Raymond to Naples. At Naples, take Route 35 north to its junction with Route 117 in the village of Harrison. Turn right on Route 117 to Twin Bridges.

GENERAL NOTES

Some exciting riffles and pools will also be found on the Crooked River above Twin Bridges. Route 35/5 travels along the river north of Lynchville. Although access is somewhat restricted, the highway crosses the river in several places, and some good fishing can be found.

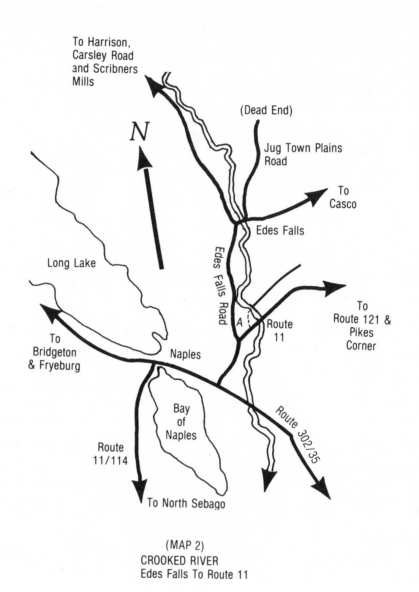

To Harrison,
Carsley Road
and Scribners
Mills

(Dead End)

Jug Town Plains
Road

N

To
Casco

Edes Falls

Long Lake

Edes Falls Road

To
Route 121 &
Pikes
Corner

A
Route
11

To
Bridgeton
& Fryeburg

Naples

Route 302/35

Bay
of
Naples

Route
11/114

To North Sebago

(MAP 2)
CROOKED RIVER
Edes Falls To Route 11

KEY
A   Mile Brook Pool Road (dirt)

THE CROOKED RIVER
Edes Falls to Route 11

GENERAL DESCRIPTION

From Edes Falls to where the Crooked River passes under Route 11 in the town of Casco, water characteristics change somewhat. While the upper reaches are largely riffled, broken by pools and deadwater stretches, the sections below Edes are largely slow water, broken by occasional riffles. Nevertheless, some excellent fishing for landlocked salmon is found here, some very productive pools and riffle spots.

Like the upper section of the Crooked, much of the river below Edes Falls is easy to wade. Steep banks prevent this in several areas, but roll casting will allow the fisherman to get his fly to a strategic location with little difficulty. The slow moving characteristic of this stretch means fishermen might do well to put in a canoe below the bridge at Edes Falls and drift slowly downstream. Some excellent "hidden" pools will be discovered this way. But caution should be exercised, especially when approaching other fishermen or spots where fish might be lying. Basically, there are two specific areas to fish on the Crooked between Edes Falls and Route 11. The first is just above and particularly just below the old mill dam at Edes Falls. In the fall fish will be found in both locations. Once the "fall run" is under way, however, action is apt to be found just about anywhere.

From the bridge at Edes Falls looking downstream a trail used to parallel the right bank. At the time of this writing, however, a house is under construction there, so fishermen should make it a point to ask permission before crossing the property. The only other way to get there is to wade the river.

The other "hotspot" on this section of the Crooked is a place called Mile Brook Pool. This is a deep, magnificent pool that is known for holding good numbers of fall fish. It is easily accessible and receives a great deal of pressure, and can only accommodate two or three fishermen at one time. However, the riffles below the pool are often productive, and there are several other pools located upstream and downstream, easily reached by trails starting at Mile Brook Pool.

BEST TIMES TO FISH

The riffles and pools below Edes Falls are among the first to receive fishing pressure each fall, since they are the first that the salmon encounter on their migration upstream. Late August starts things rolling, and action continues until the end of the season.

Contrary to popular belief, salmon do not migrate into a spawning tributary all at once, but rather in spurts, when conditions are just right. Once water levels rise and temperatures start to fall in the Crooked, salmon will move upstream, and continue to do so until the end of the season.

BEST FLIES

Those flies suggested for the other section of the Crooked River will work here as well. Remember to experiment if a fly fails to arouse attention after a fair test, and to study each pool or riffle, placing your offering properly.

HOW TO REACH EDES FALLS

From Portland, take Route 302 to North Windham, turning east on Route 11 in Naples. Travel east two miles to where the Edes Falls Road heads north; Edes Falls is approximately three miles up that road.

To reach Mile Brook Pool, continue on Route 11 one-half mile after passing the Edes Falls Road. Take the dirt road which heads off to the left just before the bridge over the river. Parking is available at the end of the road.

GENERAL NOTES

Some excellent salmon fishing pools are available below the Route 11 bridge. They are best reached by canoe, putting in at the Route 11 bridge; fishermen can then drift downstream to the bridge on Route 302.

From Route 302 downstream, there are fewer areas worthy of attention, but by putting a canoe in at the bridge, some action may be found between there and where the river meets the Songo River at the Songo Locks.

From Bolster's Mills downstream to Route 11 in Casco, the Crooked

River is restricted to fly fishing only throughout the open water fishing season. From Route 117 (Twin Bridges) downstream 400 feet to two red posts, only artificial lures may be used between June 15 and September 15. The entire Crooked River is restricted to fly fishing only between September 16 and 30; the daily bag limit on salmon, togue, and trout at this time is one fish. The daily bag limit during the rest of the season is two fish of the salmon, trout, and togue species, singly or in combination.

Finding a place to camp or lodge close to the Crooked River can be difficult. Sebago Lake State Park in Naples offers campsites, and there are several sporting camps in operation on Long Lake in Harrison. In most cases, the fisherman will have to travel a few miles each day to fish either the upper or lower section of the river as described.

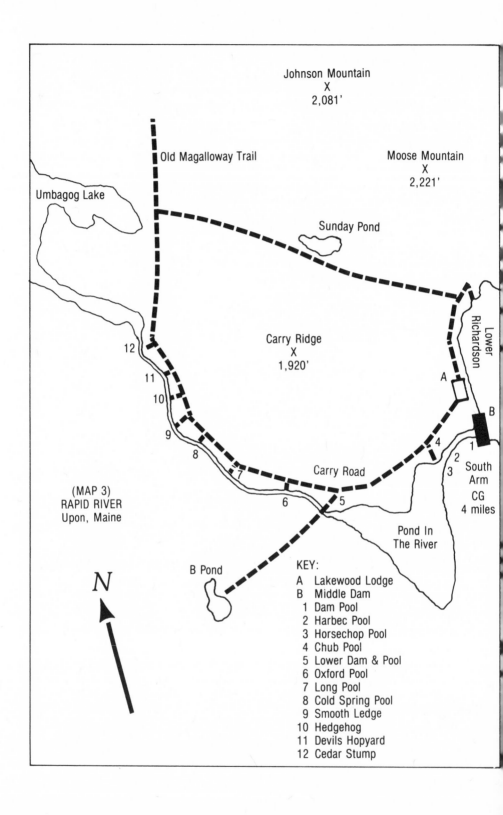

Johnson Mountain
X
2,081'

Old Magalloway Trail

Moose Mountain
X
2,221'

Umbagog Lake

Sunday Pond

Lower Richardson

Carry Ridge
X
1,920'

A

B

12

11

10

9

8

7

4

1

2

3

South
Arm
CG
4 miles

(MAP 3)
RAPID RIVER
Upon, Maine

Carry Road

6

5

Pond In
The River

N

B Pond

KEY:
A   Lakewood Lodge
B   Middle Dam
1   Dam Pool
2   Harbec Pool
3   Horsechop Pool
4   Chub Pool
5   Lower Dam & Pool
6   Oxford Pool
7   Long Pool
8   Cold Spring Pool
9   Smooth Ledge
10 Hedgehog
11 Devils Hopyard
12 Cedar Stump

THE RAPID RIVER

Lower Richardson Lake to Umbagog Lake

GENERAL DESCRIPTION

In Oxford County, Maine, 25 miles southwest, as the crow flies, of Rangeley Village, Middle Dam holds back 15-mile long Lower Richardson Lake. Starting below that dam, the fly fisherman will find one of the most challenging and unique landlocked salmon and native brook trout rivers that Maine has to offer — the Rapid River.

The river's name accurately describes its water flow and average drop per mile. From Middle Dam to a point above Umbagog Lake, a distance of only 4.5 miles, the river drops an average of 40 feet each mile, or a total of 180 feet in just over four miles! It is said that the Rapid River has one of the most severe drops of any river east of the Mississippi without a waterfall. Although much of the river is a mass of riffles, rapids, and whitewater, the fly fisherman should not think for a minute that it is worthless as habitat for coldwater gamefish.

Actually, the Rapid has some of the most consistent salmon and trout fishing in the Northeast, largely due to its drop. The gradient of this flowage keeps water temperatures relatively cool throughout the fishing season, and action will be found not only in the traditional peak months of May and June, but straight through July and August as well. Whenever I get the itch to catch landlocked salmon on dry flies during the warm weeks of summer, I head for the Rapid — and I've never been disappointed!

The Rapid is not a very large river. It averages about 30 to 35 feet in width, although some of the pools are wider. The river flows generally east to west, enters only one other body of water (Pond-In-The-River), and is partially blocked by only one ill-kept barrier (Lower Dam), between Middle Dam and Umbagog Lake. The Rapid offers some of the most interesting, challenging, and consistently productive salmon and trout pools and riffles in Maine.

BEST PLACES TO FISH

Although the Rapid River consists of much fast-moving water, there are as many as a dozen noted pools and riffle areas where the fly fisherman can wet his line. All are easily accessible from a tote road running down the north side of the river. While the "Carry Road", as it is called, doesn't always parallel the river, paths lead to major pools; most are marked. From Middle Dam to Cedar Stump, the last pool on the river before Umbagog Lake, it is approximately a one and one-half hour hike. All pools must be reached by foot, since vehicles cannot reach this side of Lower Richardson Lake.

The first pool the fisherman comes to is Dam Pool, just below Middle Dam. This is a magnificent pool of rocks, riffles, and swirling water where salmon like to lie. This is one of the most productive pools along the river. Salmon up to 12 inches will be taken readily, and specimens up to 16 inches and as large as three pounds are sometimes taken.

Dam Pool can be fished from either bank, or from many of the large rocks and boulders close to shore. Waders or hip boots could help you get to these strategic casting spots but the pool can be fished easily without them.

Harbec Pool is located just downstream and around the bend from Dam Pool. This is a large deep area — action is less productive than in Dam Pool, but some acceptable fish are taken. Horsechop Pool is located several hundred yards downstream and can hardly be found during times of high water; in low water, however, it can liberate some good salmon.

Chub Pool is the last notable pool before the river empties into Pond-In-The-River. This is a large, deep pool, and, because of the large salmon and native brook trout found there, one of my favorite areas. At the upper end of the pool is a set of rapids, and at the lower end the pool enters the pond in a riffle area. Salmon and trout will be found within the entire pool, although some exploring and study will indicate the better potential holding spots.

Below this pond the fisherman will find Lower Dam. There is a highly productive pool on both sides of this barrier; the upper pool is easily waded during periods of normal flow. The downstream pool must be fished from the bank, although restricted wading is possible short distances from shore with hip waders. Some big salmon and trout are available in both areas.

Downstream from Lower Dam are several other productive pools and rapid areas which the fisherman with extra time might want to consider. It should be understood however, that reaching them takes time — those making the hike should carry a lunch and carry a flashlight for the walk back after the sun goes down. These lower areas, because of the time and effort required to reach them, receive less fishing pressure but offer good fishing. They include Oxford Pool, Long Pool, Cold Spring Pool, Smooth Ledge (this is a great place for a swim on hot afternoons), the Hedgehog, the Devil's Hopyard, a massive set of rapids, and Cedar Stump.

BEST TIME TO FISH

As I mentioned earlier, the Rapid River is a productive salmon and trout flowage throughout the open fishing season except during periods of unusually low water. From mid-April, most pools are high with spring run-off, but casting streamers work well.

By mid-May or shortly thereafter, water levels start to recede, and small wet flies, nymphs, and dry flies begin to produce. The first hatches of May flies and caddis flies start to appear at about this time, and it is a real treat to take rising salmon on a floater. Hatches peak in June, but sporadic appearances will remain active all through the open season, particularly in the early afternoon until dusk, making July and August worthwhile periods.

When the sun is at its zenith and surface action appears to taper off, a wet fly worked just below the surface, or a dry fly allowed to drift with current and to sink just under the surface and worked upstream, will often induce a strike.

September is a highly productive time on the Rapid River. Water levels rise slightly with late rains, water temperatures cool, and fish become a little more active. Small wet flies and streamers work well, as do nymphs. But I have taken salmon on dry flies at this time, too.

BEST FLIES

Fishing the Rapid in the early spring requires the use of streamers and bucktails. Among the best producers are the Black Ghost, Gray Ghost, the Black and Yellow Marabous, the White Marabou, the Mickey Finn, the Supervisor, the Red and White, and the Ballou Special. Any streamer fly known for taking landlocked salmon is worth trying, however. Flies tied in sizes 6 through 10 are best.

For wet flies the fisherman should carry the Coachman, Hare's Ear, Leadwing Coachman, Blue Dun, Picket Pin, Woolly Worm, and Professor. Here again, the landlock often attacks on a whim, and most wet designs are apt to produce results. Some good nymph patterns include the March Brown, the Atherton Dark, the Black Nymph, the Otter Nymph, the Muskrat Nymph, the Zug Bug and Tellico, the Hendrickson and Brown Caddis Pupa. Use these in sizes 12 through 18.

The landlocked salmon inhabiting the Rapid River do not appear to be overly selective individuals. During a specific hatch, matching the color and size of the natural as closely as possible always helps, but during other periods I have received action on just about everything from the Adams right down to a Humpy or Grasshopper. Fly fishermen anticipating using floating flies should carry a good selection and, during periods when a hatch is not in progress, experiment until action starts.

Over the years, a list of my favorite dry flies has included the Adams, the Mosquito, grasshopper patterns with yellow, green, and brown bodies, the Cahill, the Royal Wulff, Quill Gordon, March Brown, Hendrickson, the Humpy with yellow, orange, or green body, the Grey Caddis, Grey Fox, the Henryville Special, the Hairwing Caddis, Blue-Wing Olive, Red Quill, Bird's Stonefly and Woodchuck Caddis, the majority of these tied in sizes 10 to 16.

HOW TO REACH THE RAPID RIVER

From Portland, Maine, take the Maine Turnpike to Gray, Exit 11. Take Route 26 through Poland Spring, Poland, Oxford, and Norway to Bryant Pond. South of the village of Bryant Pond, take Route 232 to Route 2 then left on Route 2 to its junction with Route 5 on the right. Take Route 5 to Andover and South Arm.

From South Arm it is a four-mile boat ride to Middle Dam; there is no vehicle access.

GENERAL NOTES

The only way to reach Middle Dam and the Rapid River is by boat across Lower Richardson Lake from South Arm. There is a state boat launching facility approximately a mile from the entrance to South Arm Campground. Boaters should take heed of windy weather. Lower Richardson can really get rough, and crossing the open lake can be dangerous.

The river itself is restricted to fly fishing only along its entire length throughout the fishing season. The daily bag limit from opening day to September 15 is five fish; from September 16 to September 30, the limit is reduced to one fish. All salmon must be at least 14 inches in length; brook trout must be a minimum of six inches in length.

At the present time, camping is not permitted on the west shore of Richardson Lake other than at the primitive sites operated by South Arm Campground. The main campground is situated on the "southern arm" of the lake and offers campsites with trailer and camper hook-ups, hot showers, general store, and a boat ramp. Their open season stretches from Memorial Day through September 15. Additional information may be obtained by writing South Arm Campground, (winter) c/o Mr. Ervil Kennett, North Fryeburg, Maine 04058, or (summer) South Arm Campground, P.O. Box 247, Andover, Maine 04216.

Lakewood Lodge and Camps are found within walking distance of Middle Dam and offer the only lodging accommodations on that side of the lake. The service is American Plan, and I must say that the meals served are among the best I've ever tasted at any sporting lodge. For rates and additional information, contact Mr. Stan Milton, Lakewood Lodge, Andover, Maine 04216. Lakewood Lodge provides a shuttle across Lower Richardson Lake for its clientele at no extra cost.

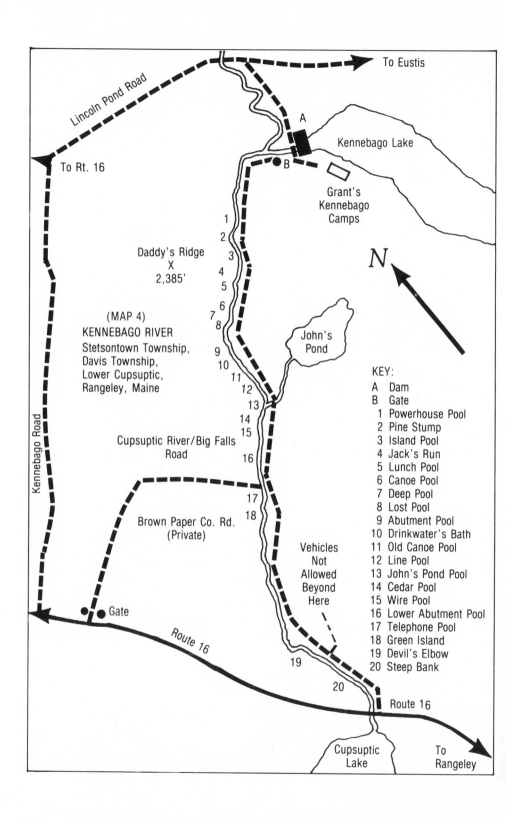

To Eustis

Lincoln Pond Road

To Rt. 16

A

Kennebago Lake

B

Grant's
Kennebago
Camps

Daddy's Ridge
X
2,385'

1
2
3
4
5
6
7
8
9
10
11
12
13
14
15
16
17
18
19
20

John's
Pond

(MAP 4)
KENNEBAGO RIVER
Stetsontown Township,
Davis Township,
Lower Cupsuptic,
Rangeley, Maine

N

Cupsuptic River/Big Falls
Road

KEY:
A   Dam
B   Gate
1   Powerhouse Pool
2   Pine Stump
3   Island Pool
4   Jack's Run
5   Lunch Pool
6   Canoe Pool
7   Deep Pool
8   Lost Pool
9   Abutment Pool
10 Drinkwater's Bath
11 Old Canoe Pool
12 Line Pool
13 John's Pond Pool
14 Cedar Pool
15 Wire Pool
16 Lower Abutment Pool
17 Telephone Pool
18 Green Island
19 Devil's Elbow
20 Steep Bank

Brown Paper Co. Rd.
(Private)

Vehicles
Not
Allowed
Beyond
Here

Kennebago Road

Gate

Route 16

Route 16

Cupsuptic
Lake

To
Rangeley

THE KENNEBAGO RIVER

Kennebago Lake to Route 16

GENERAL DESCRIPTION

Of the landlocked salmon rivers in Maine, the Kennebago is one of the most renowned. While the river is actually born in a series of small ponds located in the wilderness of Seven Ponds Townships on the Canadian border, it is the 13-mile stretch from Kennebago Lake in Stetsontown to where Route 16 crosses the river in Rangeley that is of primary interest to the fly fisherman. The river upstream from Kennebago Lake offers some excellent fishing for native brook trout. But it is the 20 or so pools downstream which receive the bulk of fishing pressure each year.

For much of its length downstream from Kennebago Lake, the Kennebago is an impressive river. It's wide enough to canoe with ease, and many fishermen choose to put in a canoe at the bridge over the river on the Lincoln Pond Road and hit the pools as they work downstream. This seems to be a good idea, since some of the better pools below the two power dams are difficult to reach on foot. Several can be reached by foot trails, but productive pools halfway downstream to Route 16 take time to locate without the aid of a canoe.

There are other access points to many of the pools along the river, however. As mentioned, most require a short (or lengthy!) hike, but the fishing at certain times can be well worth the effort.

From where the river passes under Route 16, a dirt road leads along the Kennebago's east bank, allowing vehicle access as far as Steep Bank Pool. Fishermen can park here and hike to various pools and riffles upstream via trails and the Brown Paper Company Road. The road parallels the river in many areas and it is possible to hike all the way to Kennebago Lake, fishing along the way. It should be understood, however, that this is a long trek. I prefer to find a pool or riffle of interest and spend a day fishing that one spot.

Characteristically, the Kennebago offers a variety of water conditions.

There are some pleasant riffles and moderate rapid areas interspersed with deep pools. Insect life cannot be considered over-abundant, but the river does produce some strong May fly and caddis fly hatches starting in mid-May. June sees the insect hatches at their peak, with sporadic emergences occuring through the season, often into early September. The river contains both brook trout and salmon, with the best salmon action starting in late August and continuing through September.

BEST PLACES TO FISH

From the outlet of Kennebago Lake, the fly fisherman will find many magnificent pools and riffle areas along the Kennebago all the way downstream to below Steep Bank Pool, approximately three miles north of Route 16. Many of the better known pools and fishing spots are well-defined. But in truth, action is possible just about anywhere along the river at specific times of the season. It helps if a fisherman knows where salmon and trout are apt to be lying, however. Most fishermen, even those with limited experience, will not have difficulty in recognizing potential hotspots.

From the second powerhouse below the lake to where the outlet of John's Pond enters the river, there are 13 recognized and titled pools or riffle runs. They offer a host of challenges; some are deep with restricted wading areas, others are as close to perfect as a fly caster could desire. The same is true of the riffle areas. As suggested earlier, this section of the Kennebago is best fished or reached by canoe or foot trail starting at the outlet of Kennebago Lake.

From the outlet of John's Pond to Steep Bank Pool, there are seven other well-known pools. Best reached via the old railroad bed leading to and past Steep Bank from Route 16, they, too, offer a variety of characteristics and excellent fishing. Again, however, it should be kept in mind that these pools, and those below the lake, are situated miles from any vehicle access points. Plan your day well. Pack a lunch, carry a flashlight for the hike back, and let someone know where you are going and when you plan to return.

BEST TIMES TO FISH

The Kennebago River is recognized as one of the finest "fall run" landlocked salmon rivers in Maine. It is a tributary of Cupsuptic Lake, which feeds Mooselookmeguntic, both known for their healthy salmon fisheries. Each fall, starting around the third week of August, water is released from the powerhouse below Kennebago Lake, and the rising water levels start the salmon moving upstream. Generally speaking, chances of finding fish in the river are good starting around August 15 or 20 and continuing through the close of the open season.

As far as fishermen are concerned, the height of the "run" is traditionally seen between September 10 and 20. By this time, late rains and released water have raised the river's level considerably and this, coupled with cooler autumn weather, makes for peak fishing. The lower pools, from Route 16 to John's Pond Pool, become active first and will produce fish anytime after water levels start to rise or temperatures cool. The pools and holding areas further upstream start to produce a week or so later, once salmon have had an opportunity to move. These areas are a good bet anytime after the second week of September.

Of course, certain conditions can curtail fall activity on the Kennebago — or any fall salmon river. A drought, or even slightly low water conditions, can delay migration, as can abnormal water temperatures. As a rule, however, a certain amount of water is released each September, raising water levels enough to begin the run. Fishermen traveling long distances are advised to call a guide service or knowledgeable outdoors-oriented business to obtain water conditions before heading for this river. One such outlet for information is the Rangeley Region Sports Shop. Their phone number is (207) 864-3309.

For the fisherman who doesn't consider cold weather a burden, the Kennebago offers some fine salmon and brook trout fishing in the spring. Following ice-out, huge numbers of smelt move into the river to spawn and salmon follow them to fill their stomachs after a long, hard winter. While much of the better action is found from close to Steep Bank Pool down to Cupsuptic Lake, and while water conditions are high (if the river is clear) and the weather is still bone cold, some good action is possible for the hardy enthusiast. This spring action will start to taper off by early May.

BEST FLIES

In the spring, when landlocked salmon follow the smelt into the Kennebago following ice-out, casting streamers offer the best chances for success. The Grey Ghost, Light Edson Tiger, Dark Edson Tiger, Black Ghost, Blue Smelt, and Tri-Color are among the best patterns — use sizes 4 through 8. A sinking line or sink-tip line will be needed, fished in the riffles and pools and worked to imitate smelt.

The fall fishing is somewhat different. The flies just mentioned take salmon each autumn, but the Mickey Finn, Supervisor, Red and White, Nine-Three, and Green Ghost should be carried — and tried. Streamers should be considered following a sudden rise in water levels. Nymphs and small wet flies work well, also. Although this may be nothing more than a personal observation, I have had better results with dark or natural shaded nymphs and wet flies than with bright colored patterns. The Otter and Muskrat Nymphs, Hare's Ear, and Hendrickson Nymph are among my favorites, along with the Cahill, March Brown, Hendrickson, Hare's Ear, and Leadwing Coachman wet flies. I fish them with a floating line, just beneath the surface.

Many will argue, however, that bright colored flies are best on the Kennebago, and this may be so at certain times. I've seen salmon taken in September on the Parmachene Belle, Professor, Red Ibis, and the like when anglers were doing little with other patterns. My only explanation is that one never knows for certain what will entice a fall landlock to the hook because of his feeding habits and interest in other matters. Fishermen visiting the Kennebago at this time should carry a good assortment of flies, know how and where to use them, and experiment.

HOW TO REACH THE KENNEBAGO

From Portland, Maine, take the Maine Turnpike to Auburn, Exit 12. Follow Route 4 to Turner, Livermore Falls, Farmington, and Rangeley. From Rangeley, take Route 16 west to where the Kennebago River is crossed.

The old railroad bed, now a dirt road to Steep Bank, is located on the right side of Route 16 (going west) before the bridge. To reach the pools below Kennebago Lake, cross the bridge and continue on Route 16 to the Kennebago Road that leads to Grant's Kennebago Lake Camps.

GENERAL NOTES

The Kennebago River from the second power dam downstream is restricted to fly fishing only. It opens to fishing with the general law on April 1, closing on September 30 each year. From the outlet of Kennebago Lake to the second powerhouse, the daily bag limit is five fish; from the second powerhouse downstream the bag limit is one fish.

Finding a place to camp or lodge is not difficult in this area. Camping areas are found at Haines Landing on Mooselookmeguntic and along Route 16 down to Rangeley Village. Housekeeping cabins and lodges are found everywhere. For additional information, contact the Rangeley Lake Region Chamber of Commerce, Rangeley, Maine 04970. For those fishing the upper section of the river, one of the most convenient places to stay is Grant's Kennebago Camps, located about one mile from the river. Their address and telephone number: Grant's Kennebago Camps, P.O. Oquossoc, Maine 04964, (winter) (207) 864-3754, (summer) (207) 864-3608.

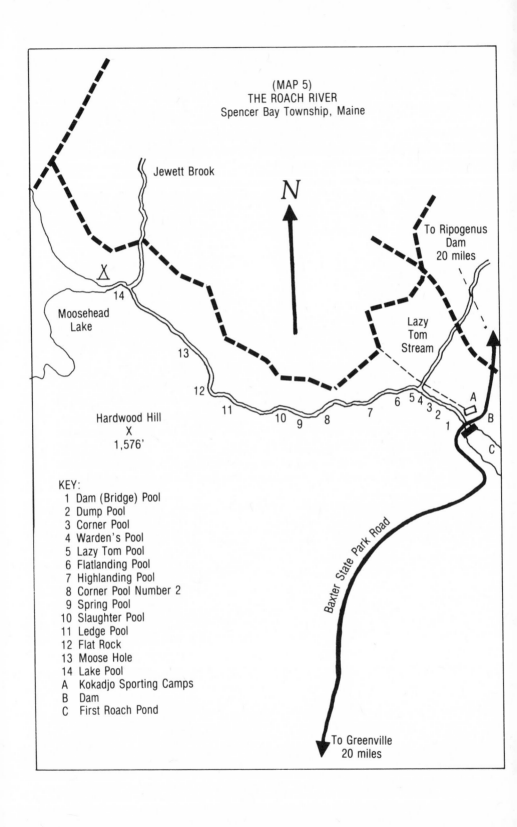

(MAP 5)
THE ROACH RIVER
Spencer Bay Township, Maine

Jewett Brook

N

To Ripogenus
Dam
20 miles

Moosehead
Lake

Lazy
Tom
Stream

14

13

12

11

10 9 8 7 6 5 4 3 2 1

A

B

C

Hardwood Hill
X
1,576'

Baxter State Park Road

KEY:
 1 Dam (Bridge) Pool
 2 Dump Pool
 3 Corner Pool
 4 Warden's Pool
 5 Lazy Tom Pool
 6 Flatlanding Pool
 7 Highlanding Pool
 8 Corner Pool Number 2
 9 Spring Pool
10 Slaughter Pool
11 Ledge Pool
12 Flat Rock
13 Moose Hole
14 Lake Pool
 A Kokadjo Sporting Camps
 B Dam
 C First Roach Pond

To Greenville
20 miles

THE ROACH RIVER

Spencer Bay Township

GENERAL DESCRIPTION

The first time I fished the Roach River a few years ago I kicked myself several times; I had passed over the bridge that crosses the river at Kokadjo many times on my way to the West Branch, but had never taken time to stop and fish it; what a mistake on my part! Since that day, I have been back a half dozen times, and with each visit my interest and enthusiasm over this flowage builds; the Roach is a unique river, with some magnificent fish.

The Roach River has its headwaters at First Roach Pond, located approximately 20 miles northeast of Greenville on the Baxter State Park Road. Much of the river is slow-moving, with few rapids or riffle areas. Yet, because it feeds Moosehead Lake, which sustains one of the finest landlocked salmon fisheries in the Northeast, the Roach is an important tributary. Like the Crooked and the Kennebago rivers, the Roach River receives large runs of fall salmon and is therefore important to fly fishermen. While many may not find it as exciting or esthetically rewarding as other rivers with substantial runs of fall salmon, it is still one of the most challenging salmon rivers I've ever had the pleasure to fish.

The fact that the river has few fast water areas, requiring the fisherman to know his adversary, and that the banks bordering the river's course are thickly covered, demanding well-executed roll casts or short backcasts, is enough to test the skills of most enthusiasts. But more than that, what pools do exist offer a varied choice of characteristics.

Several are deep, others less so, but each is different. The fisherman will have no difficulty in finding a challenge on this river — so visit the Roach during its most productive periods. You'll see what I mean.

BEST PLACES TO FISH

As I indicated earlier, the Roach River is a slow-moving waterway, broken occasionally by small riffle areas. Fishing is largely confined,

therefore, to the various pools situated downstream from the bridge and dam located on the Baxter State Park Road at Kokadjo. While action is possible in other sections of the river, one is hampered by restricted wading and by casting obstacles, and I strongly suggest that the fisherman dedicate his time to one or more of the recognized pools mentioned on Map #5, particularly those upstream from Lazy Tom Stream.

Starting at the dam, the first pool the fisherman will hit is Dam Pool, immediately below the bridge. This is a fairly deep holding area where salmon lie after making the journey upstream from Moosehead. Approximately ten minutes downstream is Dump Pool, immediately followed by Corner Pool. Three hundred yards further on is Warden's Pool, recognized by a log cabin visible from the river.

The pools just mentioned are best reached via the right-hand bank (looking downstream) over an old tote road which starts from Kokadjo Sporting Camps. Keep in mind, however, that this is a PRIVATE ROAD and PERMISSION should be sought BEFORE using it. The general store across the bridge on the right is owned by the camps, and information may be sought there. To assure access, it is suggested that you lodge at the camps, since this road is often restricted to guests only. Advance reservations are highly recommended. The Roach is a popular salmon river and accommodations are booked early.

The pools below Warden's Pool are best reached and fished from the left bank. Fishermen should cross the river below Warden's Pool, and 20 minutes downstream they will come to Lazy Tom Pool, just below where Lazy Tom Stream enters the river. Flatlander Pool is next, followed by Highlander. A further 15-minute hike brings you to Corner Pool, followed shortly by Spring Pool. Twenty minutes below Spring Pool is Slaughter Pool, the last pool accessible from the dam.

The remaining pools along the Roach start approximately two miles downstream. They are best reached by crossing the dam on the Baxter State Park Road at Kokadjo and taking the first left after passing Lazy Tom Bog; this is a dirt road. Check your odometer, travel one and one-half miles and take the next left, passing through a gravel pit. After traveling 7.2 miles, there is a tote road on the left. From this point, it is a 10-minute walk to Ledge Pool.

Downstream, the fisherman will find Flat Rock Pool, followed by the Moose Hole ten minutes away. The last pool is found just upstream from where the river empties into Moosehead Lake. This one can be difficult to reach. On my last visit, the bridge over Jewett Brook was out, making the road impassable. But the best fishing is found in the upstream pools anyway, once water levels have started to rise.

BEST TIMES TO FISH

The Roach is like any other fall salmon river, offering its best activity once water levels rise and temperatures cool. For the most part, fishing at any other time of the year other than right after ice-out and in September is a waste of time. Some excellent spring fishing is available, but considering that the West Branch is only 20 or so miles away I wouldn't give it much time since water levels can make the Roach difficult to fish. However, some big salmon are taken at this time up until water levels start to recede. Some excellent activity is also available as early as July and August if water is being released at the dam, but this is never guaranteed.

The flow on the Roach River is controlled for the most part by the dam at First Roach Pond — and by rain. During normal years, water is released sometime around the first week of September and fishing activity begins to pick up. From about the second or third week of September, once the high water is aided by cool fall weather, the fishing is great, and will continue to be so right to the close of the season. Again, however, activity is governed by water flow. If water is released in July and August, fish will move upstream and fishing will be good. If not, September is the time to try your luck. Fishermen may want to telephone Kokadjo Sporting Camps for up-to-the-minute water conditions; their number is (207) 695-2593.

BEST FLIES

During period of high water, especially after a torrential rain or a release of sufficient water from the dam, casting streamers should be used. The White Marabou, Muddler, Black Ghost, Grey Ghost and Red & White, tied on sizes 6 and 8 hooks, are suggested. Other patterns will produce action, too. Some experimenting should be done if these patterns fail to produce.

Nymphs and small wet flies work well, also. Personally, I have found success on the Black Nymph and Otter Nymphs, and have had tags on several others. The Atherton Dark Nymph, Muskrat, and Hare's Ear patterns have proven good selections with a number of fishermen.

As for wet patterns, the Olive Heron, first tied by Nick Lambrou and described in Dick Surette's "Trout And Salmon Index", has always worked well for me, especially during times of high water. The original olive body style is good, but Roach River salmon seem to prefer the same design tied in black and brown. Other personal favorite wet designs for the Roach include the Hare's Ear, Coachman, Leadwing Coachman, and Picket Pin. I've also found action on black and brown Woolly Worms, fished just under the surface. If these flies fail to produce after a fair workout, I experiment with small streamers and bucktails (depending upon water levels), or wet flies of various colors, or even nymphs.

HOW TO REACH THE ROACH

From Portland, Maine, take the Maine Turnpike to Interstate 95 in Augusta, take Interstate 95 past Waterville and exit at Newport. Take Route 7 through Dexter to Sangerville, then Route 6/15 to Greenville on the southern tip of Moosehead Lake. Entering the village of Greenville, pass the famed Indian Store and continue north approximately 20 miles on the Baxter State Park Road to Kokadjo.

GENERAL NOTES

The Roach River can be a difficult river to fish, especially the first time. Many of the pools are difficult to reach and, for the most part, the best fishing will be found from Lazy Tom Pool upstream. It is suggested that those fishing the river for the first time patronize Kokadjo Sporting Camps, fish these pools and get to know the river. In truth, when water levels are right and fish are "in", the fisherman will find all the action he wants in this section. The mailing address of Kokadjo Sporting Camps is Mr. George Midla, Kokadjo Sporting Camps, Kokadjo, Maine 04441.

From First Roach Pond to Moosehead Lake, the Roach River is restricted to fly fishing only starting May 1. From opening day to September 15 of each year, the bag limit is one salmon, two togue (lake trout), and two trout. From September 16 to September 30, the daily bag limit is only one fish.

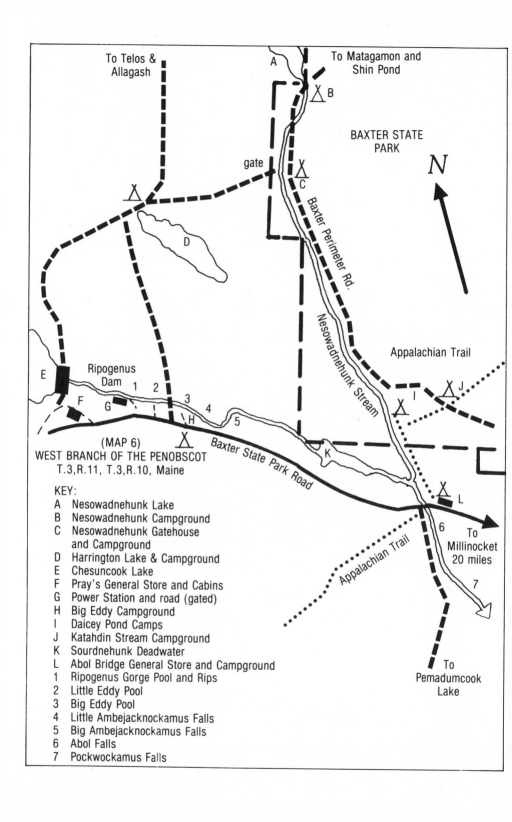

To Telos &
Allagash

To Matagamon and
Shin Pond

A

B

BAXTER STATE
PARK

N

gate

C

D

Baxter Perimeter Rd.

Appalachian Trail

Nesowadnehunk Stream

E

Ripogenus
Dam   1   2

J

F   G   3
              4
         H   5

I

(MAP 6)
WEST BRANCH OF THE PENOBSCOT
T.3,R.11, T.3,R.10, Maine

Baxter State Park Road

K

L

6

To
Millinocket
20 miles

7

Appalachian Trail

To
Pemadumcook
Lake

KEY:
A Nesowadnehunk Lake
B Nesowadnehunk Campground
C Nesowadnehunk Gatehouse
   and Campground
D Harrington Lake & Campground
E Chesuncook Lake
F Pray's General Store and Cabins
G Power Station and road (gated)
H Big Eddy Campground
I Daicey Pond Camps
J Katahdin Stream Campground
K Sourdnehunk Deadwater
L Abol Bridge General Store and Campground
1 Ripogenus Gorge Pool and Rips
2 Little Eddy Pool
3 Big Eddy Pool
4 Little Ambejacknockamus Falls
5 Big Ambejacknockamus Falls
6 Abol Falls
7 Pockwockamus Falls

THE WEST BRANCH OF THE PENOBSCOT

Ripogenus Dam to Pockwockamus Falls

GENERAL DESCRIPTION

Ask any fly fisherman which river in Maine offers the best opportunities for catching landlocked salmon — chances are he (or she) will say, "the West Branch of the Penobscot." In fact, landlocked salmon fishing and the West Branch are so closely linked with one another and receive so much attention and publicity that this magnificent flowage is considered the best salmon river Maine has to offer.

Whether or not the West Branch is indeed Maine's premier landlocked salmon river is a matter of personal judgment. I like it. I enjoy fishing it. But there are other rivers and streams I enjoy fishing equally. However, I can't argue with the fact that the West Branch has one of the healthiest resources of salmon in the Northeast — few other rivers can match the average size of Penobscot salmon.

The West Branch of the Penobscot is one of Maine's longest watersheds. Starting in a series of small remote ponds in Piscataquis County as the North Branch of the Penobscot, it is not until after the river leaves Seboomook Lake that it becomes known as the West Branch. For approximately 50 miles, the river twists and turns before finally emptying into Chesuncook Lake, the third largest lake in Maine. At the southern end of Chesuncook is Ripogenus Dam, and it is the 11.5-mile stretch of river downstream from this point which is the most popular among fishermen.

The West Branch is a very scenic river, another reason why it is so popular among fishermen. Once past Ripogenus Dam, it passes through a deep-walled gorge, tumbles over several sets of massive rapids and falls, slowing occasionally before reaching Sourdnahunk Deadwater to form some magnificent salmon holding areas. The banks are studded with hardwoods, fir, and pine, and majestic Mt. Katahdin watches over this river, visible from several places. Eagles and hawks can be seen gliding in the wind currents above the river, keeping a watchful eye out for easy prey. Moose, deer, and other wildlife are visitors to the river and inhabitants of the wilderness which surrounds it. So, the West Branch is more than just a river containing landlocked salmon and brook trout. To many, it is a piece of Maine as it was a century ago — pure, clean, unspoiled. I see it and feel it everytime I visit its shores. I go primarily to fish. But to camp on the banks of this most unique river, to be a part of its legend, makes being there special — makes you *feel* special. Few places generate that feeling today. And because of that, the West Branch is indeed special, and, in this way, the best Maine has to offer.

The landlocked salmon were first introduced to the waters of the West Branch of the Penobscot sometime in the mid-1920s. Since that time, the species has been the principal fishery resource and has done amazingly well. While examples in the six- and seven-pound class are taken on occasion, the average salmon runs between 16 and 18 inches, and close to two pounds. Smaller fish are taken, of course, quite regularly. But the chances of hooking a good-size salmon are excellent, particularly during periods of peak activity. Overall, if a fly fisherman is primarily interested in fishing for large salmon, the West Branch is the place to go.

The reasons why salmon continue to do so well in the Penobscot are linked to the river's physical characteristics. It is large compared to most other salmon rivers in Maine; in many places it is more than 100 yards wide. It is deep, with a constant current that is swift and powerful. From Ripogenus Dam to Abol Bridge, a distance of approximately 12 miles, the river drops over 300 feet — this keeps the water cool and well-oxygenated throughout the year. Feed is abundant, and even during periods of low water, there is enough water to satisfy the salmon's strict requirements. Biologically, the West Branch is ideal landlocked salmon habitat, and the fishing there proves it.

BEST TIMES TO FISH

The West Branch is not only unique in natural beauty, it is unique, too, in the sense that it is a productive salmon river throughout much of the fishing season. While activity peaks at certain times, it is very possible to find action from any riffle or pool from mid-May to the end of September.

Legally, that section of the West Branch from Ripogenus Dam downstream opens to fishing on April 1. A few hardy fishermen work the river this early, but conditions are far from ideal. Water levels are apt to be high and certain sections may still be clogged with ice. Snow still covers the ground in the north country at this time, and fishing in this region in April is a cold, often bitter, undertaking.

But some excellent salmon can be found during these first weeks of the season. As spring progresses and the water level of the river rises with snowmelt, salmon become more active and by the second week of May action is starting to increase. Conditions are still cool into middle or late May, however, and while some good fishing is possible, fishermen should be patient.

Generally speaking, the fishing season gets off to its traditional start on the West Branch on Memorial Day weekend. It is during this long holiday when the crowds arrive, and it is also at this time when the river approaches normal flow. The days are warm, and although water temperatures are still cold, fishing is excellent. The river starts to experience sporadic insect hatches at about this time, and while wet flies, streamers and nymphs continue to produce the best results, action is possible on floating flies as well. Personally, I love to fish the West Branch in June. The weather is pleasant, the black flies have not yet become a nuisance, insect hatches — May fly, caddis fly and stone fly — are active, and fishing is at its peak. The entire month of June is magnificent!

July continues to produce good fishing. Action may taper off slightly during the heat of the day, but the morning, late afternoon, and evening hours are excellent.

August is about the same, although a long, hot spell can greatly deter salmon activity. Action is good when water is released at Ripogenus Dam. Unfortunately, however, it is never known ahead of time when this will occur, so a trip cannot be planned to coincide with a water release. Visiting and fishing the river in August is still worthwhile, however. Hatches are sporadic, but when they do occur, they can be strong, creating near frenzy among the salmon. If you explore the river banks, particularly around the riffle areas, you will undoubtedly discover discarded stone fly shucks on the rocks and logs. I've had some of my best fishing on large, dark brown and black stone fly nymphs fished on the edge of the riffles.

Next to June, September is my favorite time on the West Branch, particularly after a heavy rain. The deeper pools such as Little Eddy and Big Eddy are highly active at this time, but action is apt to be found just about anywhere below Ripogenus Dam. The weather is pure pleasure, and the activity of the salmon is rewarding. September is a "must" time to visit the West Branch.

BEST PLACES TO FISH

You can generally expect action just about anywhere below Ripogenus Dam. Every pool, riffle area, or set of rapids is a potential hotspot. Many of the best sections are easily reached, if not visible, from the road, and the fisherman is advised to check any section that he can see.

Not every pool or riffle area on the West Branch below Ripogenus Dam is specifically named, but several are. Little Eddy and Big Eddy are two of the most popular spots. Little Eddy is extremely deep, set between two high rock walls; it can not be easily waded. The best way to fish Little Eddy is with a canoe anchored in mid-stream or other strategic locality.

Big Eddy is a long, deep area (site of Big Eddy Campground). Its edges can be waded from both banks. The far bank can be reached by crossing the bridge over the river on the road that leads to Telos Landing and the Allagash. A quarter-mile after crossing the river, a dirt road cuts back on the right. This road takes you to some primitive campsites owned by Pray's Camps, and to the river.

BEST FLIES

Streamers and bucktails are best on the West Branch from opening day to late May, during periods of high water (such as after a heavy rain), and from mid-September to the end of the season. I have had good luck on the Grey Ghost, Mickey Finn, Nine-Three, Black Ghost, and White Marabou. Patterns such as the Ballou Special, Joe's Smelt, Red & White, Supervisor, and Pink Lady do well, too. Other designs should be carried and used as well; those mentioned here are only a few that may produce results. Sizes 6 through 10 are best; my favorite for the West Branch is a #8.

When water levels start to recede on the West Branch, and just before insect hatches start to appear, some excellent fishing is possible on wet flies. The Gold Ribbed Hare's Ear, Coachman, Leadwing Coachman, March Brown and Light Cahill are just a few good selections. I like wet flies from size 10 to 14.

The West Branch has a consistent current and keeping a dry fly floating properly can be a test of one's skill. Because of this, I like dry flies that float high; this often calls for heavy tied patterns that are durable and bulky. While many of the favorite patterns such as the Adams, Hendrickson, Light Cahill, Grey Fox, March Brown, and Mosquito will

produce results, the Wulff dry flies, Humpys, and designs tied to imitate adult stone flies and caddis flies are extremely cooperative.

The Ausable Wulff, along with the brown, grey and grizzly Wulffs are excellent selections, as are Bird's Stonefly (brown/orange, grey/yellow), the Little Black Stone, Little Red Stone, the Hairwing Caddis tied in cream, tan, brown, pale green, and the Chuck Caddis tied in the same colors. The Henryville Special produced one of my biggest West Branch salmon in 1980, and the Grasshopper design with orange or olive body is good. A Hornburg fished on the surface can do well, too.

For nymphs, fishermen visiting the West Branch should consider the Atherton Light and Dark Nymphs, the Caddis Larvae in cream, olive, green and grey, Grey Nymph, the Otter and Muskrat patterns, the Hendrickson, Truebloods Caddis, the Tellico, Flick's Stonefly, the Brown Stone, the Little Black Stone, the Black Stone and the Montana Stone. Generally, sizes 8 to 16 are best, although some patterns may not be commercially available on certain hooks.

GENERAL NOTES

The West Branch is one of Maine's best salmon rivers — it can be highly productive, but at times it will simply refuse to give up fish. Experience is needed to get to know it and find its secrets, but I have never met a fisherman who has been there and didn't enjoy it.

The flies mentioned previously are only suggestions. Salmon will be taken on other patterns, although those mentioned are popular and will produce results. As on any river, any fly must be placed and worked properly to produce action — this is particularly true on the West Branch.

The West Branch opens to fishing legally on April 1. From Ripogenus Dam to the head of Sourdnahunk Deadwater, the river is restricted to the use of artificial lures only until September 15. The daily bag limit is not to include more than two salmon. From September 16 to 30, the same section of river is restricted to fly fishing only; daily bag limit one salmon or one trout.

From the head of Sourdnahunk Deadwater to Ambejejus Lake between April 1 and September the general law is enforced: daily bag limit not to include more than two salmon. From September 16 to September 30 this section is restricted to fly fishing only, daily bag limit one salmon or one trout.

Camping and lodging facilities along the West Branch are limited, but there is a convenient campsite at Big and Little Eddy and housekeeping cabins available close to Ripogenus Dam. There are no other facilities available to the public. The cabins and general store at Ripogenus Dam are approximately 42 miles from Greenville and 30 miles from Millinocket.

Addtional information may be obtained by writing or calling Pray's Housekeeping Cabins and Campground, Ripogenus Dam, Greenville, Maine 04441; (207) 989-3636, Ext. 671.

HOW TO REACH THE WEST BRANCH

From Portland, Maine, take the Maine Turnpike and Interstate 95 to Newport. Take Route 7 to Dover-Foxcroft, heading north on Route 6/15 to Greenville. From Greenville, take the Baxter State Park Road to Kokadjo, passing over the Roach River. Continue on to the West Branch, approximately 20 miles.

Many fishermen prefer to take Interstate 95 to East Millinocket. They then take Route 11/157 west to Millinocket, continuing on past the entrance of Baxter State Park to the West Branch. This is the best route early in the season. However, from June to the end of the season I prefer to go through Greenville. Keep in mind that the Baxter State Park Road north of Kokadjo to Ripogenus Dam is dirt. It can be traveled by most conventional vehicles, however.

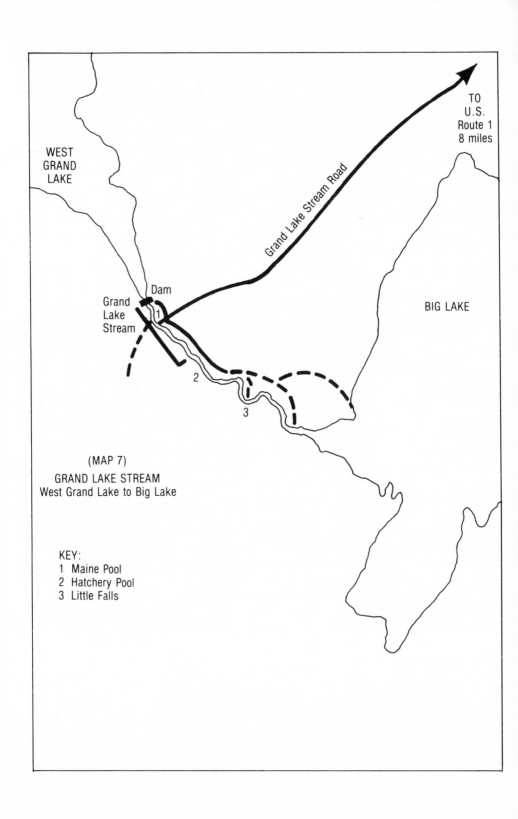

WEST
GRAND
LAKE

Grand Lake Stream Road

TO
U.S.
Route 1
8 miles

Dam

Grand
Lake
Stream

1

BIG LAKE

2

3

(MAP 7)
GRAND LAKE STREAM
West Grand Lake to Big Lake

KEY:
1 Maine Pool
2 Hatchery Pool
3 Little Falls

GRAND LAKE STREAM

West Grand Lake to Big Lake

GENERAL DESCRIPTION

While Maine is recognized as one of the best landlocked salmon states in the Northeast, few of our rivers which maintain the species are famed or renowned outside the confines of the state. The West Branch is an exception, as is the Kennebago. Nearly every other salmon river, however, is generally known only to resident enthusiasts or a limited number of non-resident fishermen who visit Maine each year.

The only other river which meets the criteria of being "famous" or "renowned" among fishermen from all states along the Eastern Seaboard is Grand Lake Stream, a relatively short river stretching just about three miles between West Grand Lake and Big Lake in Washington County.

Grand Lake Stream is simply a magnificent stretch of water. From where it leaves West Grand Lake to where it joins the waters of Big Lake, the fisherman will find a constant flow tumbling over rocky riffles and gravel bars, broken by deep pools. Although Grand Lake Stream is fairly wide, much of it can be waded during periods of normal flow, allowing the fisherman to present and work his fly tactfully. The stream is the major salmon rearing tributary of West Grand Lake, and offers some of the finest landlocked salmon fishing in Maine.

The fisherman visiting this region of Maine will soon discover that there is something special here. Not only is there great salmon fishing in the stream, but there is a certain aura surrounding the small village — one of simplicity and friendliness. The hamlet of Grand Lake Stream sits at the southern tip of West Grand Lake, bordering both banks of the stream for a short distance below the dam. The population is listed at around 200 people and the majority earn their living catering to sportsmen: hunters and fishermen as guides, camp and lodge operators, or some other sporting service. Grand Lake Stream is, always has been, and undoubtedly always will be, an outdoor recreational-oriented community.

BEST PLACES TO FISH

During periods of peak activity, the fisherman will find action just about anywhere along Grand Lake Stream. Much of the fishing pressure, however, is concentrated in three areas: Main Pool, located below the dam; Hatchery Pool, next to the Grand Lake Stream Fish Hatchery; and in the vicinity of Little Falls, found approximately two miles downstream from the village.

It should be kept in mind, however, that there are numerous spots along the stream's course which can provide excellent fishing. Many of the riffle areas and pools have no specific names; the majority can be easily reached by using the Little Falls Road, which parallels the river on the east bank. It is almost easy to fish this flowage, since many of the better sections can be seen or easily reached by roads.

BEST TIMES TO FISH

Excellent salmon fishing is possible on Grand Lake Stream from the moment ice goes out straight through to September 15, when the stream closes to fishing. Traditionally, ice leaves West Grand Lake and the stream early, considering its location. By mid-April, fishing in the stream is often possible. Water flow is high and powerful, and wading is restricted, but some good action is possible from shore.

Streamers such as the Gray Ghost, Black Ghost, Nine-Three, Goldenhead, Joe's Smelt, and Grandlaker are among the top producers. These and other patterns continue to do well during periods of high water, up to about the third week of May.

As water levels recede and temperatures start to warm a little bit, Grand Lake Stream starts to experience its insect hatches. The stream provides good May fly, caddis fly and stone fly emerges from about the third week of May through June (the principal month for the dry fly fisherman) and into July and even August if water levels do not get too low. September is often a productive time on Grand Lake Stream, too.

BEST FLIES

I have already mentioned a list of streamer flies known to produce salmon on Grand Lake Stream. For your convenience, however, they include the Gray Ghost, Black Ghost, Nine-Three, the Goldenhead, Joe's Smelt, Ranger, and Grandlaker in sizes 4 through 8. The Goldenhead, Ranger, and Grandlaker are well-known regional flies, and may be purchased at fly and tackle shops in the area.

For nymphs, I highly recommend all stone fly and caddis fly patterns; Bird's Stone fly No. 2, the Black Stone, and the Brown Stone, along with the Brown Caddis Pupa. Some other nymph patterns worth considering are the Otter and Muskrat Nymphs, the Hare's Ear, Tellico, Zug Bug, Atherton Dark, Hendrickson, March Brown, and Black Nymph. All nymphs in sizes 10 to 14 are excellent.

I like to fish Grand Lake Stream with dry flies in June and early July when surface action is at its peak. The following is a list of flies I have found cooperative: Adams, Quill Gordon, Hendrickson, Light Cahill, Mosquito, Humpy with green, yellow, or orange body, Gray Fox, Gray Caddis, Henryville Special, and Hairwing Caddis. I have also taken fish on Black Ant imitations, Woolly Worms, Royal Wulffs, and small Muddlers. Sizes 10 to 14 do well.

I would like to stress, however, that Grand Lake Stream has some impressive caddis fly hatches, particularly in late June and July. If a trip is planned at that time, it is recommended that dry caddis imitations such as Bird's Stone fly, Bucktail Caddis, and Woodchuck Caddis be carried and utilized. During these hatches, I've also had action on Grasshoppers, Royal Wulffs, and Ausable Wulffs.

GENERAL NOTES

Grand Lake Stream opens to fishing April 1 and closes September 15. The stream is restricted to fly fishing only throughout the season, with a daily bag limit of three salmon. Fishing within 150 feet of Grand Lake Stream Dam is prohibited.

As mentioned previously, Grand Lake Stream is a renowned recreational and sporting area. You will have little difficulty finding a place to lodge or rent a camp, although camping is not permitted; Grand Lake Stream is a resort area. It is recommended that advance reservations be made. Bookings during the peak of the fishing season are heavy. For information on the area's sporting camps, lodges, etc., contact the Grand Lake Stream Conservation Association, Grand Lake Stream, Maine 04637.

For your convenience, the following facilities are recommended: Grand Lake Stream Lodge and Cabins, telephone (207) 796-5584 (open from ice-out to October 30), Leen's Lodge, telephone (207) 796-5575, Hazelwood's Cottages, telephone (207) 796-5192, Colonial Sportsmen's Lodge, telephone (207) 796-2655, and Weatherby's Camps, telephone (207) 796-5558.

HOW TO REACH GRAND LAKE STREAM

Grand Lake Stream is a secluded spot in the wilds of Washington County. Driving time from Portland is approximately six hours. The quickest and best route is as follows: take the Maine Turnpike and Interstate 95 to Howland, then take Route 155 east through West Enfield and Enfield and on to Lincoln. In Lincoln, take Route 6 east to Topsfield, then turn south on U.S. Route 1 until you come to the Grand Lake Stream Road (approximately 15 miles south of Topsfield). Grand Lake Stream is eight miles west on that road.

OTHER MAINE TROUT AND SALMON WATERS

BIG OSSIPEE RIVER

GENERAL DESCRIPTION

Rapids, moderate riffles, and pools. Principal fishery is brown trout, stocked each spring. Average size, 9 to 11 inches.

BEST PLACES TO FISH

The stretch of river from Kezar Falls downstream to where the Big Ossipee meets the Saco River in the town of Cornish.

BEST TIMES TO FISH

May, with streamers and bucktails and nymphs fished deep. June, in the morning, late afternoon, and evenings, with nymphs and dry flies. July, with dry flies in the afternoon and evening, and with nymphs when surface action is not evident. August, with dry flies in the afternoon and evening, nymphs and small wet flies in the morning. September, with dry flies when a hatch is in progress, nymphs or small wet flies otherwise.

BEST FLIES

Wet Flies—Coachman, Hare's Ear, Leadwing Coachman, Blue Dun, Dark Cahill, Light Cahill, Picket Pin, Quill Gordon, Hendrickson, March Brown (sizes 8 to 14).

Streamers—Gray Ghost, Black Ghost, Mickey Finn, Thundercreek Smelt, Muddler (sizes 6 to 10).

Dry Flies—Adams, Hendrickson, Mosquito, March Brown, Light Cahill, Blue-Winged Olive, Grey Fox, Red Quill, Bird's Stone Fly, Humpy, Hairwing Caddis, Henryville Special, Woodchuck Caddis (sizes 10 to 16).

Nymphs—Hare's Ear, Otter, Muskrat, March Brown, Hendrickson, Atherton Dark, Bird's Stone Fly, Brown Stone (sizes 6 to 12).

GENERAL NOTES

Opens to fishing April 1, closes to fishing September 15. The daily limit is eight fish.

HOW TO REACH THE BIG OSSIPEE

From Portland, take Route 25 to Cornish and Kezar Falls. Route 25 crosses the river at Kezar Falls; fish from this point downstream.

WILD RIVER

GENERAL DESCRIPTION

The Wild River enters Maine from New Hampshire in Maine's section of the White Mountain National Forest. It is a typical mountain river — swift, rocky, amazingly clear, and cool throughout much of the season. Water levels can get too low for productive fishing in July and August. The principal fisheries are rainbow trout, stocked by the New Hampshire Fish and Game Department in the New Hampshire section, and native brook trout.

BEST PLACES TO FISH

From one-half mile downstream from Wild River Campground to Maine/New Hampshire border. This section is in New Hampshire and a New Hampshire fishing license is required.

There is a magnificent pool located on the border line (which I have aptly named Border Pool). It is best fished by walking downstream, crossing the river, and fishing the bank next to the dirt road. This is a deep pool, and native brook trout and rainbows can often be seen holding here.

Other good places to fish can be found from the border downstream to the Androscoggin River.

BEST TIMES TO FISH

Water levels are often high into late May. June is the best month, but good fishing continues into mid-July. September can be good if rains increase water flow.

BEST FLIES

I have had little success with dry flies on the Wild River. The river does experience some May fly hatches, although they are short and sporadic. Wet flies and small streamers produce the best — try the Hendrickson, Leadwing Coachman, Picket Pin, Blue Dun, Quill Gordon, Hare's Ear, Light Cahill, Iron Blue Dun, and March Brown. Fish them deep, casting upstream in pools, letting them drift down and mend into the current.

GENERAL NOTES

The section in Maine opens to fishing April 1 and closes September 15. The daily bag limit is eight fish. The New Hampshire section is listed under New Hampshire's general fishing law. It opens to fishing the fourth Saturday in April and closes October 15. The daily bag limit is seven fish.

HOW TO REACH THE WILD RIVER

From Portland, take the Maine Turnpike to Gray (Exit 11). Take Route 26 through Poland and Norway to Bethel. Take Route 2 west to Gilead, turning south on Route 113 to Hastings' Campground.

SANDY RIVER

GENERAL DESCRIPTION

The Sandy River is one of Maine's best brown trout rivers. It flows from the town of Madrid in Franklin County southeasterly through Phillips, Strong, and Farmington, meeting the Kennebec north of Norridgewock. The best brown trout section is from Phillips to a mile north of Farmington.

The river is stocked annually. Average size of brown trout is 11 to 13 inches.

BEST PLACES TO FISH

Route 4 north of Farmington parallels the Sandy River in many places — good fishing just about anywhere.

BEST FLIES

Wet Flies—Hare's Ear, Hendrickson, March Brown, Light Cahill, Leadwing Coachman, Blue Dun, Hendrickson Emerger, Quill Gordon, Iron Blue Dun (sizes 12 to 14).

Nymphs—Flick's March Brown, Grey Fox, Iron Blue Nymph, Atherton Light, Light Cahill, Otter Nymph, Zug Bug, Hendrickson, March Brown, Black Stone, Brown Stone, Brown Caddis Pupa (sizes 12 to 18).

Dry Flies—Adams, March Brown, Light Cahill, Hendrickson, Blue-Wing Olive, Cream Variant, Grey Fox, March Brown, Mosquito, Red Quill, Quill Gordon, Hairwing Caddis, Henryville Special, Woodchuck Caddis (sizes 10 to 16).

GENERAL NOTES

The Sandy River falls under Maine's general law regulations, although the majority of fish are taken with flies. The river opens to fishing April 1 and closes September 15. The daily bag limit is eight fish. The best times to fish the Sandy River are from mid-May through June to the first or second week of July. Low water conditions prevail after this time. September can be worthwhile if late rains raise water levels.

HOW TO REACH THE SANDY RIVER

From Portland, take the Maine Turnpike to Auburn (Exit 12) and follow Route 4 through Turner, Livermore Falls, and Farmington. Continue on Route 4 north along the Sandy River.

KENNEBEC RIVER

GENERAL DESCRIPTION

The Kennebec River drains Moosehead Lake, Maine's largest lake. It flows from the East and West outlets, located on Route 6/15 running between Greenville and Rockwood.

BEST PLACES TO FISH

Good fishing for landlocked salmon is available on the East Outlet below the dam downstream to Indian Pond. This is especially true in the spring and fall.

Some fair trout fishing is available below Harris Station on Indian Pond to the town of The Forks on Route 201, although access is restricted.

Some of the best fishing on the Kennebec is found from The Forks downstream to Wyman Lake, and below Wyman Lake Dam in Bingham. Rainbow trout (no longer stocked), brook trout, and landlocked salmon are available.

BEST TIMES TO FISH

From opening day of the fishing season to late May on East Outlet and below Wyman Lake Dam. June and September are best from Harris Station on Indian Pond to The Forks downstream to Wyman Lake.

BEST FLIES

Streamers and Bucktails—Gray Ghost, Mickey Finn, Black Ghost, Light Edson Tiger, Harris Special, Maynard's Special, Ballou Special, Cardinelle, Bingham Special, Thundercreek Smelt, Hornburg, and Muddler (sizes 6 to 8).

Dry Flies—Wulffs, Humpys, Irresistibles, Bivisibles, and stone fly imitations (size 10 to 12).

GENERAL NOTES

The East Outlet of the Kennebec is open to artificial lure only fishing from May 1 to September 15. Bag limit during this time is five fish, no more than two of which may be salmon, trout, or togue. From September 16 to September 30, this same area is open to fly fishing only — daily bag limit, one fish. The Kennebec River from Indian Pond downstream to tidewater at Augusta is open to general law fishing April 1, closing September 15. The bag limit from Wyman Lake Dam in Bingham to the uppermost dam in Madison is two fish of the trout and salmon species, singly or in combination; length limit on salmon, trout, and togue — 12 inches.

From September 16 to October 31, that section of the Kennebec River from Indian Pond to tidewater in Augusta is open to fly fishing only — daily bag limit, one fish. That section from The Forks to Wyman Lake, and below Wyman Lake downstream two miles is best at this time, offering some magnificent fall fishing.

HOW TO REACH THE KENNEBEC

To reach East Outlet, take Maine Turnpike and Interstate 95 to Newport. Take Route 7 to Dexter, then Route 23 to Sangerville. From Sangerville, take Route 6/15 through Greenville and on west to East Outlet.

To reach that section of the Kennebec from The Forks to Bingham, take the Maine Turnpike and Interstate 95 to Fairfield. Take Route 201 north to Skowhegan and Bingham. The river parallels Route 201 to The Forks.

MOOSE RIVER

GENERAL DESCRIPTION

The Moose River feeds Moosehead Lake, and is one of the lake's important salmon tributaries. It provides its best fishing in the spring and fall.

BEST PLACES TO FISH

From Brassua Lake Dam to Gilbert's Pool — this is the best salmon fishing stretch for fly fishermen on the lower Moose River. From Long Pond to Little Brassua Lake — this stretch offers some magnificent riffles and rapid areas, broken by moderately flowing current. Some of the best action is found at the head and tail of these faster areas as they drop into pools and deadwater stretches.

BEST TIMES TO FISH

Because the Moose River is a major salmon tributary of Moosehead Lake, large numbers of salmon are found running the river each spring in search of smelt, and each fall on their spawning run. Generally, from May 1 to about Memorial Day, action will be found with streamers and bucktails in the areas previously mentioned. Once the spring run is over, action slows until the fall run. The fall run is apt to start by the third week of August if rain raises water levels or water is released at Brassua Lake Dam. As a rule, fall fishing is best starting around the second week of September and lasts until the close of the season. This is true in both areas mentioned.

BEST FLIES

Streamers and Bucktails—Gray Ghost, Black Ghost, Mickey Finn,

Nine-Three, Red & White, Joe's Smelt, Marabou Matuka, White Marabou, Yellow Marabou, Supervisor, Ballou Special, Pink Lady, Chief Needahbeh, Green Ghost, Moose River, and Spencer Bay Special (sizes 4 to 8).

GENERAL NOTES

That section of the Moose River from Long Pond downstream to Little Brassua Lake opens to artificial lure only fishing April 1, with a five-fish limit. From Brassua Lake Dam downstream to Gilbert's Pool and Moosehead Lake, the open season commences May 1, allowing artificial lures only until September 15. Bag limit this time, five fish, no more than two of which may be salmon, trout, or togue. From September 16 to September 30, both sections are open to fly fishing only — daily limit, one fish; 18-inch length limit on togue.

HOW TO REACH THE MOOSE RIVER

From Portland, take the Maine Turnpike and Interstate 95 to Newport. Take Route 7 to Dexter, then Route 23 to Sangerville. From Sangerville take Route 6/15 through Greenville to Rockwood; the highway follows the river from this point. You can cross the river at Rockwood if you wish. A road turns left after crossing the bridge and parallels the river. Brassua Lake Dam can be reached via a dirt road located approximately three miles west of Rockwood. Some exploring may be needed to locate it — many of these roads are unmarked. Dirt roads also lead off Route 6/15 to the section of river between Long Pond and Little Brassua Lake.

NESOWADNEHUNK STREAM

GENERAL DESCRIPTION

Nesowadnehunk Stream is located in Baxter State Park, starting its run southward from Nesowadnehunk Lake and traveling for approximately 20 miles along the park's western boundary before entering the West Branch of the Penobscot west of Abol Bridge. Much of this stream is fishable, offering some pleasant riffles, rapids, falls, and deadwater stretches. It contains a fishery of native brook trout, except for its lower stretches which may contain a limited number of landlocked salmon. Nesowadnehunk Stream is, in my mind, one of the finest native brook trout streams (with relatively easy access) that Maine has to offer.

BEST PLACES TO FISH

Baxter Park's western perimeter road parallels Nesowadnehunk Stream north of Katahdin Stream Campground. In many places, the stream can be seen from the road, and excellent fishing is possible just about anywhere. However, the fisherman is advised to work upstream or downstream from easy access points, since such areas are fished heavily.

From Katahdin Stream Campground to the West Branch, the best way to reach Nesowadnehunk Stream is via the Appalachian Trail, which follows the stream in many places.

BEST TIMES TO FISH

From about May 15 through June and into July with small streamers and wet flies, or dry flies when the situation warrants. The stream provides excellent May fly and caddis fly hatches in June and July, and sporadic appearances occur throughout much of the season. August can be slow, except in the mornings and evenings. Two-pound trout are possible.

BEST FLIES

Streamers—Mickey Finn, Black Nose Dace, Light Edson Tiger, Warden's Worry, Cardinelle, and Bingham Special (sizes 8 to 10).

Wet Flies—Coachman, Parmachene Belle, Hare's Ear, Leadwing Coachman, Trout Fin, Scarlet Ibis, Blue Dun, Picket Pin, Woolly Worm, Hendrickson, March Brown, Black Gnat, Light Cahill (sizes 12 to 14).

Dry Flies—Adams, March Brown, Hendrickson, Light Cahill, Mosquito, Black Gnat, Grey Fox, Blue Quill, Red Quill, Pale Evening Dun, Blue-Wing Olive, Cream Variant, Green Drake, Hairwing Caddis, Woodchuck Caddis (sizes 12 to 16).

GENERAL NOTES

Nesowadnehunk Stream is restricted to fly fishing only. It opens to fishing April 1 and closes August 15. No fishing from one hour after sunset to one hour before sunrise — daily limit, five fish.

HOW TO REACH NESOWADNEHUNK STREAM

From Portland, take the Maine Turnpike and Interstate 95 north to Medway, then take Route 11/157 to Millinocket and continue on to Baxter State Park. Enter via the Togue Pond gatehouse and head for Katahdin Stream Campground (7.7 miles). Fishermen fishing the lower stretches should camp and park here and use the Appalachian Trail.

Fishermen desiring to fish the upper reaches should continue on and fish the stream as they travel along. Camping is available at Nesowadnehunk Field (within sight of the stream) or Nesowadnehunk Stream Campground, a private campground (open to the public) just outside the park.

For camping and permit information on Baxter State Park, write Reservation Clerk, Baxter State Park, Millinocket, Maine 04462, or call (207) 723-5140.

Camping information for Nesowadnehunk Lake Campground may be obtained by writing Nesowadnehunk Lake Campground, Millinocket, Maine 04462.

TROUT BROOK

GENERAL DESCRIPTION

Starting in the mountainous interior of Baxter State Park, Trout Brook

and its North and South branches travel on a north by northwest course, paralleling the perimeter road between Telos Gatehouse and Trout Brook Farm. For the fly fisherman, Trout Brook itself offers the best opportunities, particularly that stretch from where the North Branch enters the main stream to the South Branch Pond Road, a distance of approximately six miles. Within this course are a host of rapids, riffles, and deep pools containing native brook trout. The average trout runs 8 to 11 inches. The brook is easily accessible via the perimeter road, although several sections travel away from the road's view.

BEST PLACES TO FISH

Anywhere from where the North Branch of Trout Brook enters Trout Brook to the South Branch Pond Road. Trout Brook is not fished a great deal, overshadowed by the ponds in the area. Good fishing is possible just about everywhere.

BEST TIMES TO FISH

From about Memorial Day, or a week earlier, through June and July into early August. Due to Trout Brook's fast flow and rapid characteristics, temperatures stay cool late into the season. Fishing is productive until water levels get too low, usually by mid-August. Trout Brook closes to fishing on August 15, so it's safe to say that productive fishing is available througout its open season.

BEST FLIES

Wet Flies—Hare's Ear, Scarlet Ibis, Muddler, Hornburg, Hendrickson, March Brown, Light Cahill, Woolly Worm, Leadwing Coachman, Picket Pin, Blue Dun, Iron Blue Dun, Ginger Quill, Black Gnat (sizes 10 to 14).
Dry Flies—Adams, March Brown, Light Cahill, Hendrickson, Gold-Ribbed Hare's Ear, Black Gnat, Grey Fox, Iron Blue Dun, Red Quill, Whirling Blue Dun, Female Beaverkill, Grasshopper, Humpy, Gray Caddis, Henryville Special, Hairwing Caddis (sizes 12 to 16).

GENERAL NOTES

Trout Brook opens to fishing April 1, but high water prevents productive fishing until middle or late May. The stream closes to fishing August 15. There is a five-fish limit. Although the brook is open to lures, most of the fish are taken on flies. Fishermen should make arrangements to camp at South Branch Pond Campground or Trout Brook, the closest campgrounds to the brook. Information may be obtained by contacting the Baxter State Park office in Millinocket.

HOW TO REACH TROUT BROOK

From Portland, take the Maine Turnpike and Interstate 95 to Island Fall. Take Route 159 west to Patten and Shin Pond. Enter the park through the Matagamon gatehouse. It is 2.6 miles from Matagamon gatehouse to Trout Brook Farm Campground — approximately six miles to South Branch Pond Campground.

FISH RIVER

GENERAL DESCRIPTION

Fish River has its headwaters in Fish River Lake in Aroostook County. It travels generally easterly to Portage Lake, then heads north, joining the St. John River at Fort Kent. This is a fairly large river, offering some of the finest landlocked salmon fishing in northern Maine. It offers many deadwater areas, mixed with riffles and rapids. Large salmon up to four and five pounds are taken each year. The best fishing will be found in the thoroughfares between the lakes of this river, although some good opportunities will be found in its wilderness sections as well.

BEST PLACES TO FISH

The thoroughfares between Mud and Cross lakes, between Cross and Square lakes, between Eagle and St. Froid lakes, and the Fish River itself just downstream and upstream from Portage Lake.

BEST TIMES TO FISH

The Fish River and the thoroughfares connecting these lakes experience good runs of salmon in the spring and fall — fishing is best at these times. From ice-out (approximately the second or third week of May) into early June is an excellent time. These areas also produce good fishing from late August to the end of the fishing season.

BEST FLIES

Gray Ghost, Black Ghost, Mickey Finn, Nine-Three, Supervisor, Joe's

Smelt, Ballou Special, White Marabou, Yellow Marabou, Harris Special, Tri-Color, Red & White, Pink Lady, Muddler, Blue Smelt (sizes 4 to 8).

GENERAL NOTES

The Fish River and its thoroughfares open to fishing April 1. From September 16 to September 30, all areas are restricted to fly fishing only. The daily bag limit during the regular season is five fish, not more than two of which may be salmon; not more than two of which may be togue. There is a one-fish limit during the fly fishing only season in the thoroughfares.

HOW TO REACH THE FISH RIVER

From Portland, take the Maine Turnpike and Interstate 95 to Oakfield, then take Route 212 to Knowles Corner and Route 11. Take Route 11 north to Ashland and Portage. The Fish River follows Route 11 in several places north of Portage.

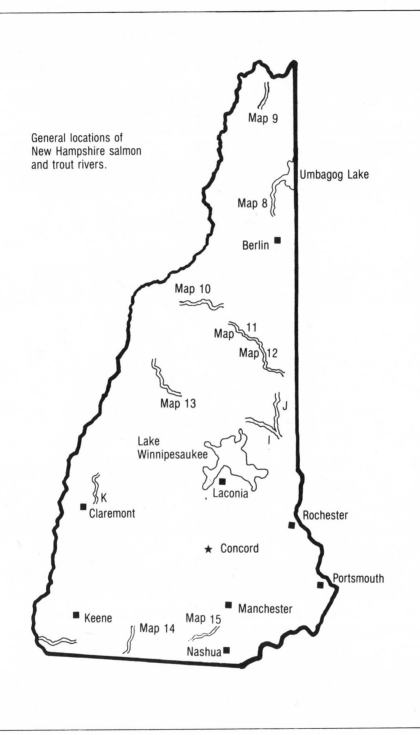

General locations of
New Hampshire salmon
and trout rivers.

Map 9

Umbagog Lake

Map 8

Berlin

Map 10

Map 11

Map 12

Map 13

J

I

Lake
Winnipesaukee

K

Laconia

Claremont

Rochester

Concord

Portsmouth

Keene

Map 15

Manchester

Map 14

Nashua

Chapter 4

The Rivers of New Hampshire

The rivers and streams of New Hampshire containing species of trout and salmon offer a mixed bag of characteristics and challenges to the fly fisherman. Those mentioned within the next few pages provide combinations of riffles, rapids, and slow stretches and, for the most part, contain fishable populations of trout and/or salmon throughout much of the fishing season.

As do its neighboring states of Maine and Vermont, New Hampshire offers the fishing enthusiast both native and stocked trout populations. For the most part, native strains are found in the waters of northern New Hampshire and in rivers and smaller streams and brooks of the White Mountains region. Generally speaking, these native trout are brook trout, plus those browns and rainbows which happen to winter over in their home stream.

By and large, however, much of New Hampshire's coldwater fishery is hatchery-oriented. Nearly one million trout of the brook, brown, and rainbow trout species are stocked annually in streams and rivers alone. These fish consist of fingerlings, one-year-olds, and two-year-olds. The breakdown, by county and species, is as follows:

BROOK TROUT*

County	Fingerlings	Yearlings	Two-year-olds
Belknap	14,600	26,650	280
Carroll	20,900	40,867	750
Cheshire	—	16,650	387
Coos	31,500	93,720	2,468
Grafton	7,836	78,360	2,689
Hillsboro	11,000	56,750	1,550
Merrimack	1,000	36,300	550
Rockingham	10,000	45,515	—
Strafford	5,000	15,480	—
Sullivan	3,300	20,950	550

RAINBOW TROUT*

County	Yearlings	Two-year-olds
Belknap	7,300	100
Carroll	17,550	525
Cheshire	6,700	100
Coos	50,800	1,361
Grafton	21,380	775
Hillsboro	26,400	300
Merrimack	18,000	830
Rockingham	30,300	2,150
Strafford	4,800	340
Sullivan	3,600	200

BROWN TROUT*

County	Yearlings	Two-year-olds
Belknap	200	—
Carroll	2,000	—
Cheshire	6,900	—
Coos	13,000	280
Grafton	6,000	—
Hillsboro	11,050	177
Merrimack	11,500	—
Rockingham	9,550	—
Strafford	500	—
Sullivan	5,100	—

*Based on 1979 stocking figures. Actual number may vary slightly from year to year.

Fishermen should keep in mind that while New Hampshire does offer some native trout fishing, those resources available from the White Mountains region south to the coast are largely stocked fish. Stocking takes place once water temperatures reach a temperature of 45°; this is usually late April or early May. Fishing generally is slow and unproductive in many rivers and streams until after this time. Waters in the White Mountains region and northern New Hampshire do not reach this temperature until approximately mid-May.

The streams of southern and central New Hampshire do, however, offer some interesting and challenging fly fishing. They are generally of freestone characteristics, providing limited insect activity in mixed riffles, small rapids, and deadwater runs. Fishing is productive from the time trout are stocked through June and into mid-July, or until water levels and temperatures get to the point where activity drops off.

During my visits to the streams of southern and central New Hampshire, I have discovered that wet flies, small streamers, and nymphs are by far the best offerings. Dry flies will produce action during a specific insect hatch, but even then small wet patterns, emerger patterns, and wet flies fished just under the surface produce more results.

The streams of northern New Hampshire and the White Mountains regions are quite different than southern waters. While many provide freestone characteristics, they offer more riffle areas, stronger rapids, and fewer deadwater sections; there are exceptions, of course. Insect life is more pronounced, and when emerges occur they are stronger and longer. Dry fly fishing is exciting and can be most challenging at specific times. And while fishing starts late in this region due to the flow of many rivers and streams, trout and salmon are cooperative in smaller flowages into mid-July, while the larger rivers such as the Upper Connecticut and the Androscoggin continue to produce fish throughout much of the fishing season.

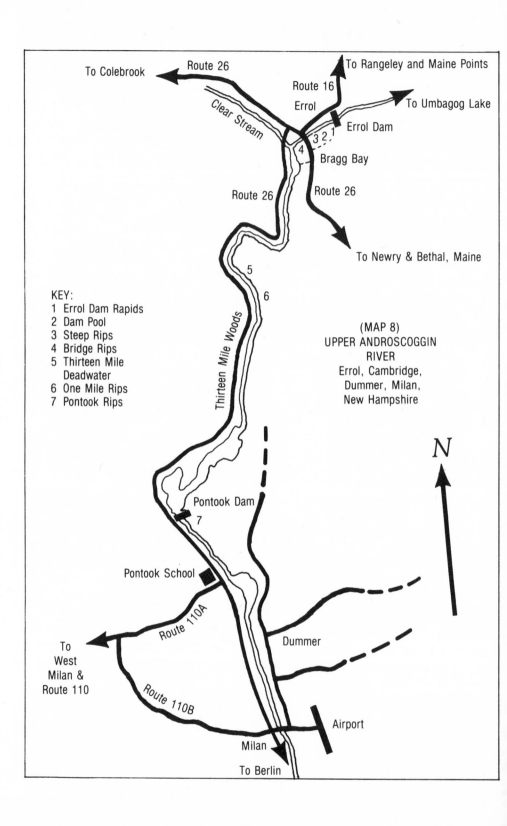

To Colebrook

Route 26

To Rangeley and Maine Points

Route 16

Errol

Clear Stream

To Umbagog Lake

Errol Dam

3 2 1

4

Bragg Bay

Route 26

Route 26

To Newry & Bethal, Maine

5

6

KEY:
1 Errol Dam Rapids
2 Dam Pool
3 Steep Rips
4 Bridge Rips
5 Thirteen Mile
  Deadwater
6 One Mile Rips
7 Pontook Rips

Thirteen Mile Woods

(MAP 8)
UPPER ANDROSCOGGIN
RIVER
Errol, Cambridge,
Dummer, Milan,
New Hampshire

N

Pontook Dam

7

Pontook School

Route 110A

Dummer

To
West
Milan &
Route 110

Route 110B

Airport

Milan

To Berlin

THE ANDROSCOGGIN RIVER

Erroll to Milan

GENERAL DESCRIPTION

The Androscoggin River is one of New Hampshire's finest trout waters. The fishery consists of brook trout, rainbows, and browns — the last species attracting the principal interest. Examples up to six and seven pounds are taken each year, although smaller fish (12 to 15") are the average. Landlocked salmon are also available.

Being one of New Hampshire's larger rivers, the Androscoggin is challenging, but not difficult, to fish. The best section for the fly fisherman lies from Errol downstream to the uppermost section of Pontook Deadwater above Pontook Dam in Dummer. This section is wide and deep in many areas, with a consistent current and generally difficult wading. It does, however, contain the best insect life and the largest amount of fish.

BEST PLACES TO FISH

Good fishing is available on the Androscoggin from the dam in Errol to Pontook Dam in Dummer. The best landlocked salmon fishing will be found in the Bragg Bay section in Errol. This is a large, wide, and deep area, and a small boat or canoe is needed to reach the best holding areas.

For browns, rainbows, and brook trout, fly fishermen should center their attention on that stretch of river located in what is known as Thirteen Mile Woods. The river is flat in this section for approximately four miles south of Errol, broken by a short series of rapids just before Thirteen Mile Woods ends. This is magnificent trout water, with huge, strong May fly and caddis fly hatches. Many areas can be waded, although the fisherman should take his time and be careful.

BEST TIMES TO FISH

The Androscoggin River legally opens to fishing January 1, but fishermen start to really spend time here starting about the third week of

April. The high water, which lasts until about mid-May, is excellent for landlocked salmon fishing. Good fishing is available right straight through the season, which ends October 15, although activity may slow up a bit in August. It is worthwhile fishing the Androscoggin anytime, however.

BEST FLIES

For landlocked salmon—Streamers and bucktails, including Grey Ghost, Black Ghost, Joe's Smelt, Nine-Three, Harris Special, Mickey Finn, Maynard's Special, Ballou Special, Winnipesaukee Smelt, and White Marabou (sizes 6 to 8).

For browns, brookies, and rainbows—Dry flies, including Adams, Quill Gordon, Hendrickson, Grasshopper, Humpy, Gray Caddis, Gray Fox, Henryville Special, Hairwing Caddis, Blue-Wing Olive, Wulffs, Hare's Ear, Woodchuck Caddis, Bucktail Caddis, and Bird's Stone fly (sizes 10 to 16).

Wet Flies—Hare's Ear, Light Cahill, March Brown, Hendrickson, Blue Dun Hendrickson Emerger, Leadwing Coachman, and Picket Pin (sizes 10 to 14).

Nymphs—Tellico, Hare's Ear, Otter Nymph, Muskrat Nymph, Zug Bug, Atherton Dark, March Brown, Hendrickson, Black Stone, Brown Stone, Brown Caddis Pupa, Green Caddis Pupa, Green Caddis Larva, Hellgrammite, Black Nymph, Bird's Stonefly No. 2, and Surette's Androscoggin Green Caddis in sizes 10 down to 16.

GENERAL NOTES

As previously mentioned, the Androscoggin River opens to fishing January 1, closing October 15. That section of the river from Errol Dam to two red markers in Bragg Bay is restricted to fly fishing only with a two-fish (12-inch length) limit. That section of the river downstream from Bragg Bay is open to lure fishing.

HOW TO REACH THE ANDROSCOGGIN

From Berlin and points south, take Route 16 north through Milan. The Androscoggin parallels Route 16 north of Milan.

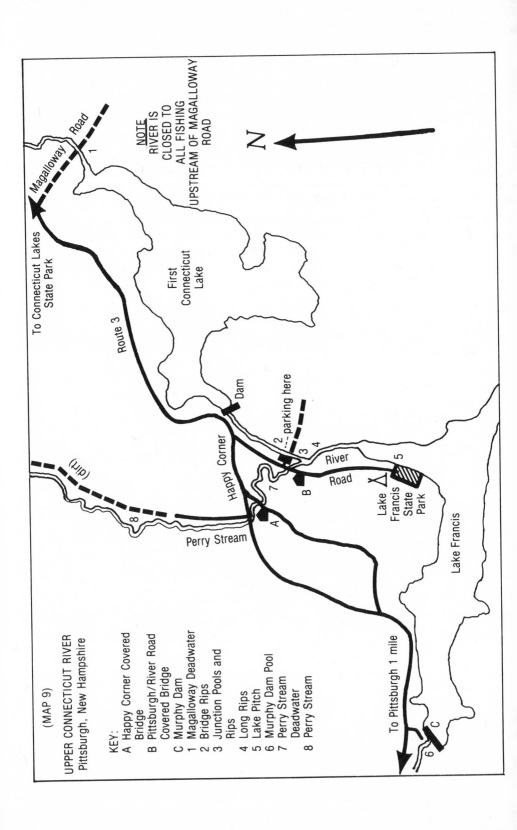

(MAP 9)

UPPER CONNECTICUT RIVER
Pittsburgh, New Hampshire

KEY:
A Happy Corner Covered
   Bridge
B Pittsburgh/River Road
   Covered Bridge
C Murphy Dam
1 Magalloway Deadwater
2 Bridge Rips
3 Junction Pools and
   Rips
4 Long Rips
5 Lake Pitch
6 Murphy Dam Pool
7 Perry Stream
   Deadwater
8 Perry Stream

NOTE
RIVER IS
CLOSED TO
ALL FISHING
UPSTREAM OF MAGALLOWAY
ROAD

N

Magalloway Road

To Connecticut Lakes
State Park

Route 3

First
Connecticut
Lake

Dam

parking here

Happy Corner

River

Road

(dirt)

Perry Stream

Lake
Francis
State
Park

Lake Francis

To Pittsburgh 1 mile

THE UPPER CONNECTICUT RIVER

Magalloway Mountain Road to Murphy Dam

GENERAL DESCRIPTION

The northern extremity of New Hampshire is a sportsman's paradise. It is a land of fir and pine, of rolling hills and clean lakes. It is a region of New England where a sportsman, whether fisherman or hunter, feels comfortable, at home — at ease.

Running through this magnificent region is the beautiful and fish-filled Connecticut River. Starting as a small trickle at Third Connecticut Lake, the river runs southward until blocked by a dam on Route 3 which forms Second Connecticut Lake. It then tumbles down through a rock gorge and wooded valley until blocked by yet another dam, this one forming First Connecticut Lake. From this point the Connecticut retains its small river characteristics and runs in a mass of riffles, rapids, and moderately flowing current to Lake Francis, formed by Murphy Dam in the town of Pittsburg.

From a fly fisherman's viewpoint, the Connecticut River is a trout and salmon utopia. There are many riffle and rapid stretches connected by moderately flowing runs, providing some magnificent and unique challenges. Insect life is well-defined and hatches are strong and consistent, with sporadic later appearances occurring throughout much of the fishing season. The river contains excellent populations of brook trout in its faster sections, as well as browns and rainbows; landlocked salmon are available in the spring and fall. Browns up to five and six pounds are not uncommon below Murphy Dam.

Fishing the Connecticut, and being in the country through which it flows, are pure pleasure. It reminds me a great deal of the Rangeley area in Maine; a clean and still pure land of fir and conifers, of fresh-flowing rivers and friendly people, of outdoor atmosphere. I enjoy visiting and fishing this northern New Hampshire river and you will, too.

BEST PLACES TO FISH

For landlocked salmon: Magalloway Deadwater, downstream from the bridge on the Magalloway Road to First Connecticut Lake. Also, from First Lake Dam downstream to Lake Francis. Excellent riffle and rapid stretches abound in this section.

For browns: From First Connecticut Lake downstream to Lake Francis and below Murphy Dam, downstream to Pittsburg. The largest browns along the Connecticut are taken below Murphy Dam and for 1.5 miles downstream.

For brook trout and rainbow trout: From First Connecticut Lake Dam downstream to Lake Francis. Good rainbow fishing also below Murphy Dam.

While fishing that section of the Connecticut River from First Connecticut Lake Dam to Lake Francis, it is recommended the fisherman take some time to fish Perry Stream. Good brown trout are available in the lower stretches below Happy Corner Covered Bridge; native brook trout are available in the upper stretches.

BEST TIMES TO FISH

The best landlocked salmon fishing on the upper Connecticut River occurs from the time the season opens in the spring (late April) through mid-May, then starting again about the second week of September and continuing to the end of the fishing season. The Connecticut experiences a strong run of salmon right after ice-out, and again in the fall. Fall fishing can be detained several days or even weeks due to low water conditions, but October fishing is generally excellent.

For browns, rainbows, and brook trout, excellent fishing is available through much of the fishing season. The best brook trout fishing occurs primarily in the spring, however.

In May, the river is high with run-off water, but by Memorial Day, water conditions will start to normalize. June is excellent with the principal hatches appearing; July is good, too. August can be slow, particularly during years of low water, but some good fishing is still available, especially in the faster stretches and below Murphy Dam. September and October can be highly productive for all species.

BEST FLIES

For landlocked salmon, try Grey Ghost, Black Ghost, Joe's Smelt, Nine-Three, Mickey Finn, Harris Special, Maynard's Marvel, Ballou Special, Golden Demon, Thunder Creek Smelt, Red & White, White Marabou Muddler, and Marabou Matuka (sizes 4 to 8).

Wet flies for trout: Hendrickson, Cahill, March Brown, Hare's Ear, Professor, Olive Heron, Leadwing Coachman, Hornburg, Muddler, Blue Dun, Picket Pin, Woolly Worm, Quill Gordon, Coachman, and Iron Blue Dun (sizes 10 to 14).

Dry flies for trout: Hare's Ear, March Brown, Light Cahill, Dark Cahill, Hendrickson, Pale Evening Dun, Whirling Blue Dun, Red Quill, Gray Fox, Ginger Quill, Mosquito, Quill Gordon, Adams, Cream Variant, Blue-Winged Olive, Gray Wulff, Bird's Stone Fly, Humpy, Grasshopper, Bucktail Caddis, Hairwing Caddis, Henryville Special, and Woodchuck Caddis (sizes 10 to 16).

Nymphs: Tellico, Zug Bug, Hare's Ear, Otter Nymph, Muskrat Nymph, March Brown, Hendrickson, Black Stone, Bird's Stone Fly No. 2, Brown Stone, Yellow Stone, Brown Caddis Pupa, Blue Quill Nymph, Hendrickson Nymph, Gray Nymph, and Atherton Light and Dark Nymphs (sizes 10 to 16).

GENERAL NOTES

That section of the Connecticut River from Second Lake Dam downstream to the upper side of the bridge on the Magalloway Road is closed to all fishing. That section of river downstream from the same bridge to First Connecticut Lake, however, is open, and offers good salmon and trout fishing as indicated.

The Connecticut River from First Connecticut Lake Dam downstream to Lake Francis is open to fly fishing only from April 1 to September 30 for salmon, and from the fourth Saturday in April to October 15 for trout. Daily creel limit is two trout and two salmon (15-inch minimum length limit on salmon, 12-inch minimum length limit on trout).

Perry Stream is restricted to fly fishing only from Happy Corner Covered Bridge downstream to the Connecticut River. It opens to fishing the fourth Saturday in April and closes October 15.

Finding a place to camp or lodge is not a problem while fishing the Connecticut River. Camps, lodges, and state parks are located nearby. Lake Francis State Park and Connecticut Lake State Forest, which borders Route 3 north of First Connecticut Lake, both provide camping facilities.

Lodges and camps are available in the village of The Glen and in several spots along Route 3 north of Pittsburg. For your convenience the following establishment is recommended: Young's Mountain View Cabins, Pittsburg, NH, telephone (603) 538-6305.

HOW TO REACH THE CONNECTICUT RIVER

From Gorham, New Hampshire, take Route 16 north through Berlin to Errol (fish the Androscoggin along the way!). From Errol, take Route 26 east to Colebrook, then take Route 3 north to Pittsburg and the Connecticut River. From Lancaster, New Hampshire take Route 3 north to Pittsburg.

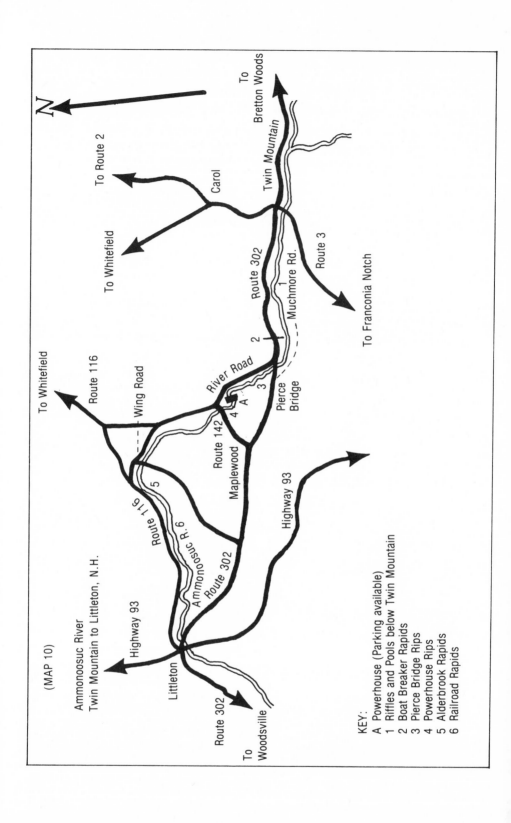

(MAP 10)

Ammonoosuc River
Twin Mountain to Littleton, N.H.

N

To Route 2

To Whitefield

Carol

Route 302

Muchmore Rd.

Route 3

To Twin Mountain

To Bretton Woods

To Franconia Notch

To Whitefield

Route 116

Wing Road

River Road

Pierce Bridge

Route 142

Maplewood

Highway 93

2

1

3

4 A

Highway 93

Route 116

Route 116

Ammonoosuc R. 6

Route 302

5

Littleton

Route 302

To Woodsville

KEY:
A Powerhouse (Parking available)
1 Riffles and Pools below Twin Mountain
2 Boat Breaker Rapids
3 Pierce Bridge Rips
4 Powerhouse Rips
5 Alderbrook Rapids
6 Railroad Rapids

THE AMMONOOSUC RIVER

Twin Mountain to Littleton

GENERAL DESCRIPTION

The beautiful Ammonoosuc River is born high in the Presidential Range of the White Mountains in Lake of the Clouds. Its uppermost reaches, upstream from the village of Twin Bridges, are a mass of fast rapids, riffles, and quick water of crystalline quality. Native brook trout are available, also rainbow and brown trout in the lower portions.

From Twin Bridges downstream, the Ammonoosuc widens and deepens, taking on the characteristics of a large stream. By the time the river reaches the city of Littleton, it has grown into a medium-sized river, a full 50 yards wide in places, with a slow to moderate current.

The best trout fishing on the Ammonoosuc is found from Twin Bridges downstream to Route 16 four miles east of Littleton. The river flows through a pleasant valley with relatively easy access facilities at several points. Within this stretch are several sets of rapids and riffle areas, with slower stretches offering moderate current where a wet fly, streamer, nymph, or dry fly can be worked productively. Overall, the river drops approximately 43 feet to the mile between these two settlements, giving the fisherman an idea of the water flow.

Unfortunately, however, while the Ammonoosuc offers some excellent trout fishing, it also suffers from low water conditions during the middle of the fishing season. It is greatly influenced by water running down from the mountains and hills, and during the warmer weeks of summer, water levels can be quite low. On the other hand, a week of rain can increase water flow to fishable levels, so the river is worth checking anytime during the season.

BEST PLACES TO FISH

Some of the best fishing on the Ammonoosuc will be found immediately downstream from the bridge in Twin Bridges. It is mostly riffle water and offers good trout habitat during times of normal flow. A little over two miles below Twin Bridges, the river comes within sight of

Route 302, offering access; the riffles and rapids continue past this point.

Another stretch to consider is Boat Breaker Rapids, upstream from Pierce Bridge. These can be best reached by turning left on to Muchmore Road immediately after crossing the steel bridge. The rapids right under this bridge produce some good fishing as well.

Some of the best trout water is found below Pierce Bridge. There is a dam two miles downstream, forming a deep backwater, but some interesting riffles are found upstream from this point off the River Road.

The river below the old dam is a mass of riffles and rapids for approximately 150 yards — then the river slows before speeding up again for Powerhouse Rapids. The river continues in a run of rapids and fast riffles until passing under a bridge on Route 142 in Maplewood. The Ammonoosuc continues in such fashion until meeting Route 116 east of Littleton. Two sets of rapids, Alder Brook Rapids and Railroad Rapids, offer powerful current and good fishing. Some excellent trout fishing is available just about anywhere in the area from Twin Bridges downstream.

BEST TIMES TO FISH

The Ammonoosuc starts to reach good fishing levels in mid-May. By Memorial Day, water flow can still be high but good fishing is generally available. June is the principal month, with good possibilities running into mid-July. The principal hatches of May fly and caddis fly species appear during this period. Good fishing is possible in August, but only after a couple of days of rain; otherwise, water levels are too low. Some good fishing is possible in September if rain increases water flow.

BEST FLIES

Wet flies: Hendrickson, Cahill, March Brown, Hare's Ear, Muddler, Leadwing Coachman, Coachman, Picket Pin, and Quill Gordon (sizes 10 to 14).

Dry flies: Adams, Cahill, March Brown, Woodchuck Caddis, Henryville Special, Hairwing Caddis, Humpy, Bird's Stone Fly, Red Quill, Mosquito, Hendrickson, Grey Fox, Green Drake, Cream Variant, and Blue-Wing Olive (sizes 12 to 16).

GENERAL NOTES

The Ammonoosuc opens to fishing the last Saturday in April and closes October 15. It is *not* restricted to fly fishing only. The daily bag limit is seven trout or five pounds. Camping and lodging facilities are available in many places along Route 302 from Twin Bridges to Littleton.

HOW TO REACH THE AMMONOOSUC RIVER

From Conway, New Hampshire, take Route 16 north to Glen, then take Route 302 through Crawford Notch State Park, through Twin Mountain to Pierce Bridge. The River Road forks right at Pierce Bridge and parallels the river to Maplewood Bridge. The Wing Road continues straight along the river.

From Concord, New Hampshire, take Route 93 north through Franklin and Franconia Notch State Park. Take Route 3 north to Twin Mountain, then head west on Route 302.

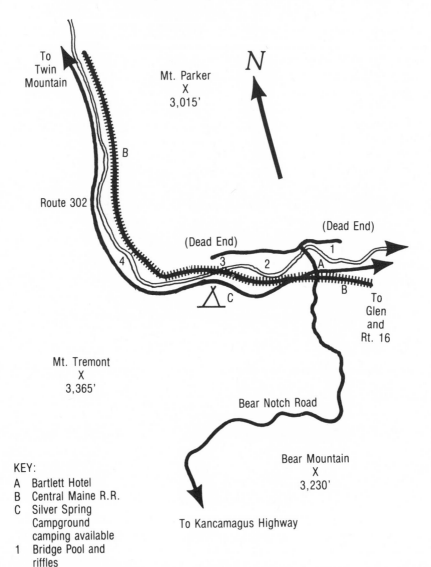

(MAP 11)
SACO RIVER
Bartlett, New Hampshire

To
Twin
Mountain

Mt. Parker
X
3,015'

N

Route 302

B

(Dead End)

(Dead End)

1

4

3

2

A

C

B

To
Glen
and
Rt. 16

Mt. Tremont
X
3,365'

Bear Notch Road

Bear Mountain
X
3,230'

KEY:
A   Bartlett Hotel
B   Central Maine R.R.
C   Silver Spring
    Campground
    camping available
1   Bridge Pool and
    riffles
2   Deep Pools
3   Railroad Bridge
4   Riffles and pools above
    Sawyer's General Store

To Kancamagus Highway

THE SACO RIVER

Bartlett

GENERAL DESCRIPTION

The Saco River is one of northern New England's longest rivers, arising from Saco Pond high in Crawford Notch, New Hampshire. Its upper reaches are typical of a fast-flowing mountain-born river, tumbling over rocks and boulders and broken only occasionally by a deep pool. The water is crystal clear and cold throughout the year.

For the fly fisherman, the Saco has very little to offer until about a mile or so upstream of Bartlett. Here the river slows a little, offering interesting riffles and deep pools containing rainbow and brook trout. Fish do not run large (up to thirteen inches or so), but it is "fun" fishing and *can* offer a challenge. This section of the Saco is worth fishing if you're passing through this section of the White Mountains or vacationing nearby. Insect life is limited due to water flow and cold water temperatures. But insect hatches of May fly and caddis fly do appear once water temperature rises over the 50° mark, usually sometime in June.

BEST PLACES TO FISH

The Saco parallels Route 302 in many places north of Bartlett. To reach some of the better riffles and pools, turn right off Route 302 at Bartlett Motel. This road crosses the river one-half mile further on; there is an interesting pool below this bridge. Take a left after crossing the bridge; this road parallels the river for two miles to a dead end. Some interesting fishing is possible downstream from Bartlett but access is greatly restricted.

BEST TIMES TO FISH

Late May and June are the principal periods. Some good fishing is possible in July as well, and even August can produce some good fish in the riffle areas and deep pools. September until the close of the fishing season is often a productive period, although it can be cold and chilly in the high country.

BEST FLIES

Wet flies: Hare's Ear, Cahill, March Brown, Muddler, Blue Dun, Dark Cahill, Picket Pin, Leadwing Coachman, Quill Gordon, Coachman, Professor, Ginger Quill, Hendrickson, Blue Dun, and Gray Hackle (sizes 10 to 14).

Dry flies: Adams, March Brown, Cahill, Mosquito, Quill Gordon, Gray Fox, Red Quill, Gold-Ribbed Hare's Ear, Hendrickson, Grasshopper, Humpy, Gray Caddis, Cream Saco Caddis, Henryville Special, Saco, Red Quill, Blue-Wing Olive, Hairwing Caddis (sizes 12 to 16).

GENERAL NOTES

The Saco River opens to fishing the fourth Saturday in April and closes October 15. The daily bag limit is seven fish or five pounds. This section is *not* restricted to fly fishing only, although that is the most popular method.

Camping is available at Silver Spring Campground on Route 302 west of Bartlett on the Saco River. Lodging is available in cabins, motels, and hotels in Bartlett.

HOW TO REACH THE SACO RIVER AT BARTLETT

From North Conway, New Hampshire, take Route 16 north to Glen, then take Route 302 west to Bartlett, approximately seven miles.

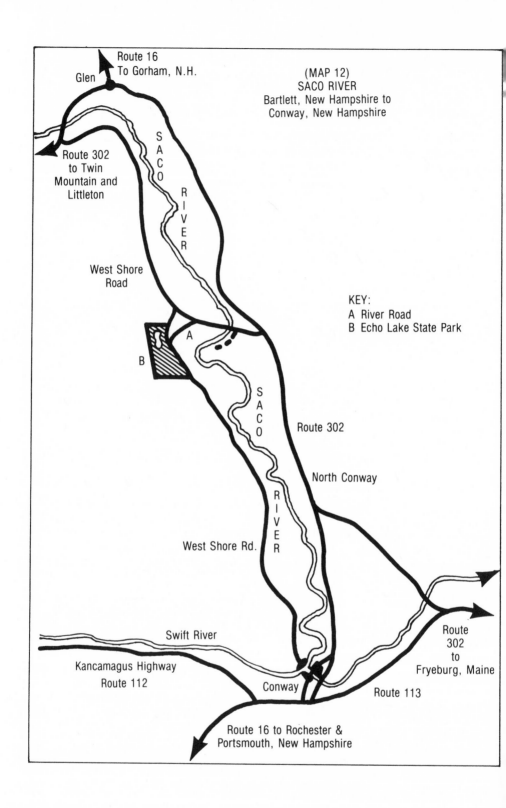

(MAP 12)
SACO RIVER
Bartlett, New Hampshire to
Conway, New Hampshire

Route 16
To Gorham, N.H.
Glen

SACO RIVER

Route 302
to Twin
Mountain and
Littleton

West Shore
Road

KEY:
A River Road
B Echo Lake State Park

A

B

SACO RIVER

Route 302

North Conway

West Shore Rd.

Swift River

Kancamagus Highway
Route 112

Conway

Route 302
to
Fryeburg, Maine

Route 113

Route 16 to Rochester &
Portsmouth, New Hampshire

SACO RIVER

Bartlett to Conway

GENERAL DESCRIPTION

Approximately six miles east of Bartlett, the Saco River passes under Route 302. From the covered bridge (visible from the modern steel bridge) downstream, the river widens and takes on the characteristics of a larger river. It is deep in several deadwater sections, and quite wide. But there are many riffles and short rapid stretches of interest to the fly fisherman. Brown trout, brook trout, and rainbows are available (browns up to two pounds or more possible at certain times).

Personally, I prefer this particular stretch of the Saco River. It is less congested by swimmers, and although it is a popular canoeing section, sharing the river with paddlers is never a problem. From what I've seen, this section receives less fishing pressure than the northern section, except during specific periods of the season. The scenery is beautiful, and the river itself is esthetically rewarding and a pure pleasure to fish.

BEST PLACES TO FISH

In many places, the Saco River south of Route 302 parallels what is known as the West Shore Road and access to some of the better fishing pools and riffles is virtually unrestricted. This is especially true from Route 302 south to the River Road in Conway. There are some magnificent riffle runs and pools in this stretch — many challenging opportunities; a fisherman can spend an entire day fishing this particular section with rewarding results.

From the River Road south, however, access is greatly restricted. The river twists and turns, swinging away from the West Shore Road, and much of the land between the road and river is private and/or posted. Access to one good spot is available on the River Road itself, approximately one-half mile west of where the River Road joins Route 16 at North Conway. Parking is available on a dirt road (blocked to vehicle access), and fishermen may walk downstream to some very nice pools and riffle areas. This section is highly recommended.

BEST TIMES TO FISH

This section of the Saco is apt to produce good fishing throughout the fishing season. However, from mid-May through early July, and from September to the end of the fishing season, are the prime periods of activity. The river offers good hatches of May flies and caddis flies in June and early July, with sporadic emerges occurring through the summer.

BEST FLIES

Wet flies: Blue Dun, Leadwing Coachman, Picket Pin, March Brown, Light Cahill, Hendrickson, Quill Gordon, Grey Hackle, Hare's Ear, Professor, Female Beaverkill, Woolly Worm, and Iron Blue Dun (sizes 10 to 14).

Streamers: Black Nose Dace, Mickey Finn, Tri-Color, Light Edson Tiger, Harris Special, Maynard's Special, Black Ghost, Muddler, Hornburg, and Golden Demon (sizes 8 to 10).

Dry flies: Adams, March Brown, Hendrickson, Light Cahill, Red Quill, Blue-Wing Olive, Cream Variant, Grey Fox, Quill Gordon, Humpy, Bird's Stone Fly, Hairwing Caddis, Woodchuck Caddis, Henryville Special, Grasshopper, Gray Caddis, Cream Saco Caddis, Saco Red Quill (sizes 10 to 18).

Nymphs: March Brown, Hendrickson, Atherton Dark Nymph, Bird's Stone Fly No. 2, Black Stone, Brown Stone, Yellow Stone, Brown Caddis Pupa, Grey Fox Nymph, Iron Blue Nymph, Otter Nymph, Muskrat Nymph, and Light Cahill Nymph (sizes 12 to 16).

GENERAL NOTES

That section of the Saco River from Route 302 downstream opens to fishing the fourth Saturday in April; it closes October 15. Much of the river is open to general law fishing. However, that section starting at two red posts located 300 yards downstream from the bridge on the River Road in North Conway to two red posts at the mouth of Mill Brook in Conway is restricted to flies and artificial lures, with a daily creel limit of two trout (12-inch minimum length limit).

Camping and lodging facilities are located in both North Conway and Conway.

HOW TO REACH THE SACO RIVER SOUTH OF ROUTE 302

From Conway, take Route 16 to Glen, then take Route 302 west until you cross the Saco at the covered bridge. The River Road takes an immediate left off Route 302 after crossing the river and parallels the river after a short distance. The River Road will be found approximately four miles south, turning to the left. It will cross the river a mile distant; Route 16 and North Conway will be found one-half mile further on.

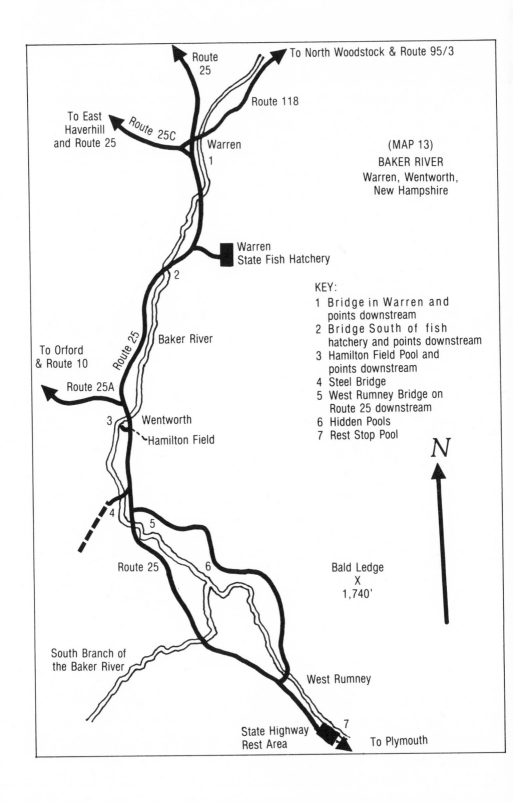

Route
25

To North Woodstock & Route 95/3

Route 118

To East
Haverhill
and Route 25

Route 25C

Warren
1

(MAP 13)
BAKER RIVER
Warren, Wentworth,
New Hampshire

Warren
State Fish Hatchery

2

KEY:
1 Bridge in Warren and
  points downstream
2 Bridge South of fish
  hatchery and points downstream
3 Hamilton Field Pool and
  points downstream
4 Steel Bridge
5 West Rumney Bridge on
  Route 25 downstream
6 Hidden Pools
7 Rest Stop Pool

Baker River

Route 25

To Orford
& Route 10

Route 25A

3

Wentworth

Hamilton Field

N

4

5

Route 25

6

Bald Ledge
X
1,740'

South Branch of
the Baker River

West Rumney

State Highway
Rest Area

7

To Plymouth

THE BAKER RIVER

Warren to West Rumney

GENERAL DESCRIPTION

In my estimation, the Baker River is the finest trout stream that the White Mountain section of New Hampshire has to offer. Starting high in the rugged White Mountain country north of Warren, New Hampshire, the Baker is a fast-flowing, rock- and boulder-infested stream until it enters the town of Wentworth. From this point south to West Rumney, its characteristics change from those of a fast-flowing mountain stream to those of a leisurely flowing river of moderate size. It retains its crystal clear water, however, remains relatively cool (up to the low 60s), and manages to maintain fishable levels through much of the fishing season. Brook trout and rainbow trout are available in the higher elevations, while browns and rainbows make up a large percentage of the fishery downstream from Wentworth.

I enjoy fishing the Baker River. Its many riffle areas and deep pools are a challenge to fish, and I've seldom been bothered by crowds of enthusiasts there. At present, it is a trout river of little note among fishermen unfamiliar with this section of New Hampshire, but among those who know it, it is considered one of the premier rivers of central New Hampshire.

Once leaving mountainous terrain, the Baker River travels through a pleasant wooded valley, passing through some villages and past some houses scattered along its banks. During periods of normal flow, it is quite wadeable, and considering the fact that it twists away from rural settlements and highways, the fisherman will find many hidden pools and productive riffle stretches after only short hikes. The Baker offers excellent May fly and caddis fly hatches; dry fly fishing is excellent (brown trout have been known to reach lengths of 14 and 15 inches!). Good opportunities are also available for those who prefer to use nymphs and wet flies.

BEST PLACES TO FISH

Route 25/118 journeys along the Baker River south of Warren to

Wentworth. This section is generally fast-flowing over a rock bottom, but fishing for brookies and rainbows can be excellent anywhere along this stretch.

At Wentworth, the river passes under Route 25 and slows somewhat. Fishermen can drive right to the bank of the river by entering Hamilton Recreation Field. Drive past the baseball diamond to a stand of pines. Upstream, the Route 25 bridge over the river will be seen with a pleasant riffle and deep pool. Some good rainbow fishing is possible here. From this point, the fisherman can wade downstream a considerable distance, fishing the pools, undercut banks, and riffles as he goes.

Approximately one and one-half miles south of Wentworth, a dirt road leads to the right and crosses the river via a narrow steel bridge; the fisherman may have to explore for this road, since it is unmarked, but some good fishing is available here. The current is slow to moderate, but the first time I fished there, I experienced a magnificent caddis fly hatch and had no difficulty rising rainbow and brown trout with correct floating imitations. It is wadeable here.

Route 25 crosses the Baker River once again a mile or so south of this point. The river twists away and back within sight of the highway until finally leaving it altogether. Those pools and riffle areas visible from the highway are worth considering, but some of the more productive sections are away from the highway. Many of these areas require hiking on the part of the fisherman, but due to the fact that they are situated back from the highway, they receive less fishing pressure and activity is noticeably better — the fishing can be well worth the effort.

Of particular interest and challenge to me were the pools and riffles in the vicinity of where the South Branch of the Baker River enters the mainstream of the Baker. I call these Hidden Pools. A hike downstream is required from the point where the river can be seen from Route 25 to reach these pools, but chances are you will find some interesting water. A fisherman can spend an entire day fishing this section, as he can those sections upstream.

Another section to consider on the Baker is accessible from the New Hampshire rest stop, located on the left side (going south) of Route 25 one-half mile north of West Rumney. The river is shallow here during periods of normal flow, with a moderate current, but some fair fishing is possible. Due to its easy accessibility, however, it is fished heavily. Some interesting riffles and pools will be found by hiking upstream and downstream from this rest area, however.

BEST TIMES TO FISH

The water flow in the Baker is influenced by run-off water from the White Mountains — thus it can remain high into mid-May. As a rule, however, it can be fished by then, and productive trout fishing continues into June (the principal month) and through July. August can offer low water conditions, but fair possibilities are available in the many riffle areas and deep pools, particularly those away from the highways. September can be interesting, as can the days right to the close of the season. In truth, the Baker is worth fishing anytime throughout the season.

BEST FLIES

Wet Flies: Hendrickson, March Brown, Light Cahill, Hare's Ear, Quill Gordon, Female Beaverkill, Coachman, Leadwing Coachman, Picket Pin, Iron Blue Dun, Hendrickson Emerger, and Muddler (sizes 10 to 14).

Dry Flies: Adams, Cream Variant, Blue-Winged Olive, Red Quill, March Brown, Quill Gordon, Grey Fox, Hendrickson, Light Cahill, Gray Caddis, Gold-Ribbed Hare's Ear, Whirling Blue Dun, Humpy, Hairwing Caddis, Henryville Special, Woodchuck Caddis, and Grasshopper (sizes 12 to 16).

Nymphs: March Brown, Light Cahill, Bird's Stone Fly Nymph No. 2, Zug Bug, Tellico, Otter Nymph, Hendrickson, Black Stone, Brown Caddis Pupa, Gray Fox, Iron Blue, and Trueblood Caddis Nymph (sizes 10 to 16).

GENERAL NOTES

The Baker River opens to fishing the fourth Saturday in April. It closes to all fishing October 15. The daily bag limit is seven fish or five pounds. The Baker is *not* restricted to fly fishing only.

Camping facilities are available at several campgrounds located on or near Route 25 in West Rumney.

HOW TO REACH THE BAKER RIVER

From Concord, New Hampshire, take Route 93 north to Plymouth, then take Route 25 west to Rumney Depot and Rumney; the Baker River parallels Route 25 in many places.

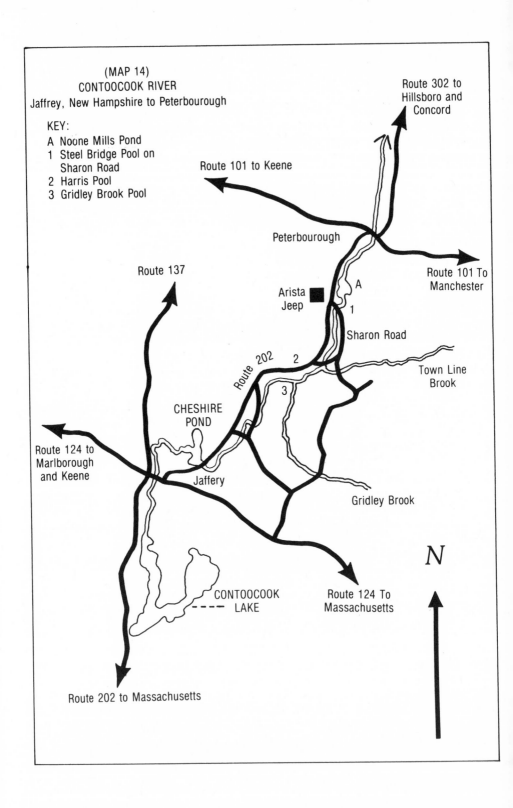

(MAP 14)
CONTOOCOOK RIVER
Jaffrey, New Hampshire to Peterbourough

KEY:
A Noone Mills Pond
1 Steel Bridge Pool on
  Sharon Road
2 Harris Pool
3 Gridley Brook Pool

Route 302 to
Hillsboro and
Concord

Route 101 to Keene

Route 137

Peterbourough

Arista
Jeep

A

1

Route 101 To
Manchester

Sharon Road

Route 202

2

3

Town Line
Brook

CHESHIRE
POND

Route 124 to
Marlborough
and Keene

Jaffery

Gridley Brook

N

CONTOOCOOK
---- LAKE

Route 124 To
Massachusetts

Route 202 to Massachusetts

THE CONTOOCOOK RIVER

Jaffrey to Peterborough

GENERAL DESCRIPTION

There are few rivers in the southwestern corner of New Hampshire that offer a fair quality trout fishery. One that does, however, is the Contoocook, particularly that stretch from Cheshire Pond in Jaffrey to what is known as Noone Mills Pond in Peterborough, a distance of approximately five miles.

The upper section of the Contoocook is not an overly large river and cannot be considered a high quality trout stream. However, much of its course is slow riffle-type water flowing over a freestone bottom. And it does offer some deep pools to challenge the fisherman. The river is stocked annually with rainbow and brown trout, and although much of the fishery is a put-and-take situation, some fish (mostly browns) do manage to survive the winter — reaching lengths of 14 and 15 inches; such fish are rare, however.

The Contoocook does have possibilities, however, and a hopeful future. The Contoocook Valley Chapter of Trout Unlimited recently undertook a stocking program with the hopes of establishing a self-sustaining trout fishery of reasonably good quality. More than 650 brown trout ranging from 11 to 12 inches in length were released in 1981 — annual stockings will continue. It is possible that such efforts will establish an excellent trout resource sometime in the future. It is questionable whether the Contoocook's water flow in August will be able to sustain such a fishery, since temperatures do get quite warm, resulting in low water. However, with stream improvements and a regulated water flow at several dams, there is reason to hope.

At the present time, the Contoocook does provide a limited trout fishery and it is worth the expenditure of some time, at least in the Jaffrey or Peterborough area.

BEST PLACES TO FISH

Generally speaking, there are three sections on the upper Contoocook where the fly fisherman is advised to concentrate his efforts. The first two spots are accessible via the Sharon Road, which leaves Route 302 south of Peterborough. Section 1 is from the first steel bridge which crosses the Contoocook downstream to Noone Mills Pond. This is largely slow-moving water broken by an occasional riffle.

The second stretch is from Harris Pool, found at the second bridge on the Sharon Road, downstream. This is riffle water and holds good trout. The fisherman should park at the stone bridge and fish the riffles and pools upstream and downstream.

The third stretch is from Cheshire Pond downstream to the Sharon Road. Various unmarked roads lead to and across the river, and the fisherman will have to explore to find them. They lead off Route 202 north of Jaffrey, with only short runs to the river. The river is narrow and generally shallow in this section, but worth spending time on.

BEST TIMES TO FISH

Early May through June and into early July in most sections. From mid-July to early August in the deep pools and riffle sections. September can be productive after rain increases water flow and cools water temperatures; October to the close of the fishing season is a good period as well.

BEST FLIES

The Contoocook has some strong May fly and caddis fly hatches, but even during periods of an emergence, little interest is devoted to them by the trout. At such times emerger patterns, hackleless dry flies, and small wet flies worked just under the surface produce the best results. At other times, wet flies and streamers and bucktails do well; the Contoocook has large numbers of baitfish, and trout seem to prefer them to insect life.

Streamers and bucktails: Black Nose Dace, Golden Darter, Silver Minnow, Muddler, Gray Ghost, and Whitlock Sculpin (sizes 4 to 8).

Nymphs: Gold-Ribbed Hare's Ear, Black Stone, Brown Stone, Little Green Stone, Brown Caddis Pupa, Green Caddis Larva, March Brown, Black Nymph, and Bird's Stone Fly No. 2 (sizes 4 to 8).

GENERAL NOTES

The Contoocook River from Contoocook Lake in Jaffrey to Peterborough is open to fishing year round. The daily bag limit is seven fish or five pounds. Lodgings are available in Jaffrey and Peterborough.

HOW TO REACH THE CONTOOCOOK RIVER

From Nashua, New Hampshire, take Route 101 west to Peterborough. From Peterborough, take Route 202 south to Sharon Road (near Arista Jeep dealership).

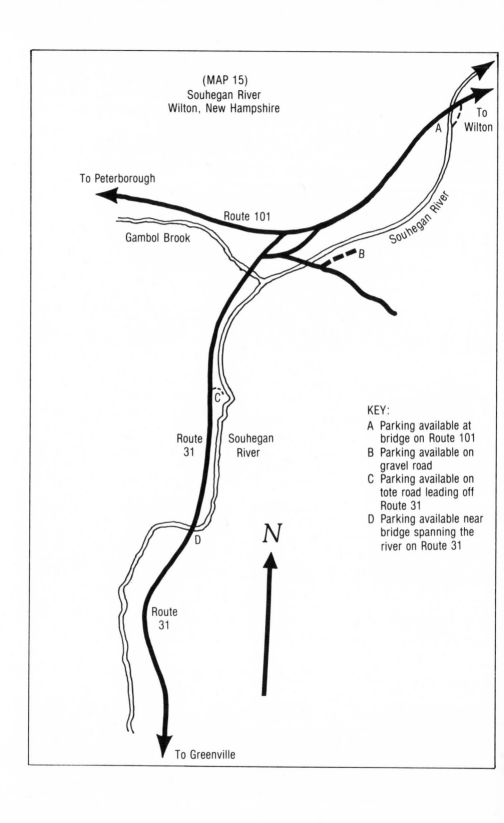

(MAP 15)
Souhegan River
Wilton, New Hampshire

To Wilton

A

To Peterborough

Route 101

Gambol Brook

Souhegan River

B

C

Route
31

Souhegan
River

N

D

Route
31

To Greenville

KEY:
A Parking available at
   bridge on Route 101
B Parking available on
   gravel road
C Parking available on
   tote road leading off
   Route 31
D Parking available near
   bridge spanning the
   river on Route 31

SOUHEGAN RIVER

Greenville to Route 101 in Wilton

GENERAL DESCRIPTION

The Souhegan River is a small watershed, rising in the rolling hills near Ipswich, New Hampshire. It flows generally northward, passing through Greenville on its way to Wilton and Milford. In its lower stretches, the Souhegan is wide and deep and offers little to the fisherman. It is the upstream section, from Greenville to Route 101 west of Wilton, that offers the best trout possibilities.

This section of the river is a series of riffles and moderate rapids, broken by short, slow-moving stretches. The banks are well wooded, offering shade and protection, and at specific times, fishing for brook, brown, and rainbow trout is excellent.

Like many of the smaller trout streams of southern New Hampshire, however, the Souhegan suffers from low water once warm weather arrives. The fishery is primarily a put-and-take situation, although a small winter-over fishery is available, providing some fish up to 13 and 14 inches.

BEST PLACES TO FISH

The best stretch of trout water on the Souhegan River is parallel to Route 31 between Greenville and Route 101, from Gambol Brook downstream to the bridge on Route 101 west of Wilton.

Access off Route 31 is limited. Several tote roads and a picnic area offer access to the river in this vicinity, and the fisherman is advised to park and work the hidden pools and riffles located upstream and downstream from these access points.

One productive spot is located under the bridge on Route 101; another is a riffle area which can be reached off a road leading from a spur between Route 31 and Route 101 (see map). From this point downstream to the bridge on Route 101, the river is all riffles and moderate rapids where brown trout and rainbow trout may be taken with dry or wet flies (at specific times).

BEST TIMES TO FISH

Early May through June with wet flies and dry flies. July can be good *if* sufficient water is available. August is usually slow, except in riffle stretches and deeper pools. September until the close of the fishing sea-son is good only if rain increases water flow.

BEST FLIES

Wet Flies: March Brown, Light Cahill, Hendrickson, Muddler, Coach-man, Leadwing Coachman, Ginger Quill, Picket Pin, Gold-Ribbed Hare's Ear, and Iron Blue Dun (sizes 10 to 14).

Dry Flies: Adams, March Brown, Light Cahill, Red Quill, Hendrick-son, Gold-Ribbed Hare's Ear, Pale Evening Dun, Quill Gordon, Gray Fox, Blue-Wing Olive, Hairwing Caddis, Henryville Special, Humpy, and Woodchuck Caddis (sizes 10 to 16).

GENERAL NOTES

The Souhegan River opens to fishing the fourth Saturday in April, and closes October 15. The daily bag limit is seven fish or five pounds. Lodging is available in Wilton and Milford.

HOW TO REACH THE SOUHEGAN RIVER

From Nashua, New Hampshire, take Route 101 west through Milford to Wilton, then take Route 31 south towards Greenville until you cross the river; fish from this point downstream to the bridge on Route 101 in Wilton.

OTHER NEW HAMPSHIRE TROUT STREAMS

BEARCAMP RIVER

GENERAL DESCRIPTION

The Bearcamp River has its source in Bearcamp Pond in Sandwich. For much of its journey to Ossipee Lake in Freedom, it is a narrow, swift-moving waterway offering some fine brook trout and rainbow trout fishing. Limited brown trout fishing is available here, also. Below Whittier, the Bearcamp widens and slows somewhat, still broken occasionally by riffles, rapids, and falls. Some excellent landlocked salmon fishing is available in the river's lower stretches in the fall.

BEST PLACES TO FISH

For brook trout, from Bearcamp Pond in Sandwich to South Tamsworth. For rainbow trout, from South Tamsworth to West Ossipee. For brown trout, from Whittier to West Ossipee. For landlocked salmon, from West Ossipee to Ossipee Lake in Freedom.

BEST TIMES TO FISH

For trout species, early May through June. For landlocked salmon, September to end of season.

BEST FLIES

Wet flies for trout — March Brown, Light Cahill, Blue Dun, Leadwing Coachman, Picket Pin, Red Quill, Hendrickson, Iron Blue Dun, Gray Hackle, Gold Ribbed Hare's Ear (sizes 10 to 14).

Dry flies for trout — Adams, March Brown, Light Cahill, Hendrickson, Gold-Ribbed Hare's Ear, Whirling Blue Dun, Red Quill, Blue Dun, Gray Fox, Hairwing Caddis, Henryville Special (sizes 12 to 16).

Streamers for landlocked salmon — Gray Ghost, Mickey Finn, Black Ghost, Nine-Three, Harris Special, Golden Darter (sizes 4 to 8).

GENERAL NOTES

The Bearcamp River opens to the taking of trout the fourth Saturday in April and closes October 15; there is a seven-fish or 5-pound daily creel limit.

The open season on landlocked salmon runs from April 1 to September 30. The daily bag limit is two salmon.

HOW TO REACH THE BEARCAMP RIVER

From Portland, Maine, take Route 25 west through Center Ossipee, New Hampshire to West Ossipee. Route 25 parallels the Bearcamp in many places west of there.

From Concord, New Hampshire, take Route 93 north to New Hampton then take Route 104 east to Meredith, then take Route 25 north to Whittier and West Ossipee.

CHOCORUA RIVER

GENERAL DESCRIPTION

The Chocorua River has its headwaters in Chocorua Lake in Tamsworth. Generally, it is riffles and rapids for its first few miles, slowing as it heads south to its confluence with the Bearcamp River at West Ossipee. Its upper reaches contain brook trout and rainbow trout. Its lower stretches (upstream from the Bearcamp to approximately Route 113) contain landlocked salmon late in the season.

BEST PLACES TO FISH

For brook trout and rainbow trout, from Chocorua Lake in Tamsworth to confluence with Bearcamp River in West Ossipee. For landlocked salmon, from Route 113 in Tamsworth downstream to confluence with Bearcamp River in West Ossipee.

BEST TIMES TO FISH

For brook trout and rainbow trout, from early May through June into early July. August can be slow due to low water except in deep pools and riffles stretches. September through the end of the season can be excellent in pools and riffle sections once rains raise water levels and temperatures cool.

BEST FLIES

Wet flies for trout — March Brown, Light Cahill, Blue Dun, Leadwing

Coachman, Picket Pin, Red Quill, Hendrickson, Iron Blue Dun, Gray Hackle, and Gold-Ribbed Hare's Ear (sizes 10 to 14).

Dry flies for trout — Adams, March Brown, Light Cahill, Hendrickson, Gold-Ribbed Hare's Ear, Whirling Blue Dun, Red Quill, Blue Dun, Gray Fox, Hairwing Caddis, and Henryville Special (sizes 12 to 16).

Streamers for landlocked salmon — Gray Ghost, Black Ghost, Mickey Finn, Nine-Three, Harris Special, and Golden Darter (sizes 4 to 8).

GENERAL NOTES

The Chocorua River opens to trout fishing the fourth Saturday in April, closing October 15. The daily creel limit is seven fish or five pounds. The season on landlocked salmon opens April 1, ending September 30. The daily bag limit is two fish.

Camping facilities are available at several campgrounds located on Route 16 in Tamworth and in White Lake State Park, also in Tamworth.

HOW TO REACH THE CHOCORUA RIVER

From Portland, Maine, take Route 25 west to Center Ossipee, then go north on Route 25/16 to West Ossipee. From West Ossipee, take Route 16 north to White Lake State Park and the town of Chocorua.

NORTH BRANCH, SUGAR RIVER

GENERAL DESCRIPTION

The North Branch of the Sugar River, also known as the Croydon River, is formed by a series of small brooks and streams in the hill country of Grantham, New Hampshire. It flows generally southward, passing through the town of Grantham, Croydon, and Croydon Flat, finally emptying into the Sugar River in Newport.

For much of its length, the North Branch is narrow, flowing through agricultural lands and wooded valleys. It is a pleasant little river, offering riffles, rapids, small falls, and interesting pools. The North Branch offers good to excellent fishing for brook and rainbow trout; there is also a limited brown trout fishery in lower stretches, but brook trout and rainbow trout made up the bulk of my catch during recent visits.

BEST PLACES TO FISH

Fair to good trout fishing is available anywhere on the North Branch

of the Sugar River from Grantham downstream to the Sugar River in Newport. The best stretch, however, runs from Croydon downstream to Croydon Flat, a distance of approximately four miles. This stretch features fairly fast-moving water with excellent riffles and rapids, broken by deep pools. It provides May fly and caddis fly hatches, but small wet flies and streamers take more fish. The river can be *seen* from Route 10 in several places, but tote roads *cross* the river and provide access to some hidden riffles and pools.

BEST TIMES TO FISH

Mid-May through June into July. August can bring low water, but action will still be available from Croydon downstream to Croydon Flat in the many riffle stretches. September can be productive, too.

BEST FLIES

Wet flies — March Brown, Light Cahill, Muddler, Red Quill, Hendrickson, Blue Dun, Grey Hackle, Leadwing Coachman, Picket Pin, Coachman, Hare's Ear, Female Beaverkill, and Ginger Quill (sizes 10 to 14).

GENERAL NOTES

The North Branch of the Sugar River is restricted to fly fishing only from the Croydon/Grantham town line downstream to where it passes under Route 10 in Croydon Flat. Other sections in Grantham and downstream from Croydon Flat are open under the general law. The season opens the fourth Saturday in April, closing October 15. The daily bag limit is seven fish or five pounds. (SPECIAL NOTE: Some interesting fishing can be found on the Sugar River from the town of Wendell west to the Claremont townline. Brook trout, rainbow trout, and brown trout are all available.)

HOW TO REACH THE NORTH BRANCH OF THE SUGAR RIVER

From Concord, New Hampshire, take Route 89 and 9 west to Henniker, then take Route 114 west to Bradford, then Route 103 to Newport. From Newport, take Route 10 north to Croydon Flat and the river.

THE ASHUELOT RIVER

GENERAL DESCRIPTION

The Ashuelot River flows from Ashuelot Pond in the town of Washington, New Hampshire, southward through the towns of Marlow, Gilsum, Surry, Keene, Swanzey, and Winchester, finally entering the Connecticut River at Hinsdale (on the Vermont border). For much of its length below Gilsum, it is a large river, and the most important section for the fisherman lies upstream from Gilsum to Marlow.

Within this particular stretch, the Ashuelot offers riffle areas, slow to moderately moving eddies, and deep pools. In places it is wide, in other sections less so — but some interesting and fine trout fishing is available.

BEST PLACES TO FISH

From Marlow, New Hampshire downstream to Gilsum, New Hampshire, a distance of approximately seven miles.

BEST TIMES TO FISH

Early May through June into early July. Also from September (if rain increases flow) to the end of the fishing season.

BEST FLIES

Wet flies — March Brown, Light Cahill, Dark Cahill, Hendrickson, Red Quill, Quill Gordon, Blue Dun, Muddler, Grey Hackle, Leadwing Coachman, Coachman, and Hare's Ear (sizes 10 to 14).

Dry flies — Adams, March Brown, Hendrickson, Hare's Ear, Whirling Blue Dun, Pale Evening Dun, Mosquito, Gray Fox, Cream Variant, Red Quill, Henryville Special, and Hairwing Caddis (sizes 10 to 16).

Nymphs — Hare's Ear, Tellico, Quill Gordon, March Brown, Hendrickson, Gray Nymph, Otter Nymph, Black Stone, Brown Stone, Little Yellow Stone, and Brown Caddis Pupa (sizes 8 to 16).

GENERAL NOTES

The Ashuelot River opens to fishing the fourth Saturday in April, closing October 15. The daily creel limit is seven fish or five pounds. Some large browns are available — some weighing more than a pound have been taken from the slower stretches.

HOW TO REACH THE ASHUELOT RIVER

From Nashua, New Hampshire, take Route 101 west to Keene, then take Route 10 north along the Ashuelot River to Gilsum and Marlow.

From Concord, New Hampshire, take Route 9 west to Keene then go north on Route 10.

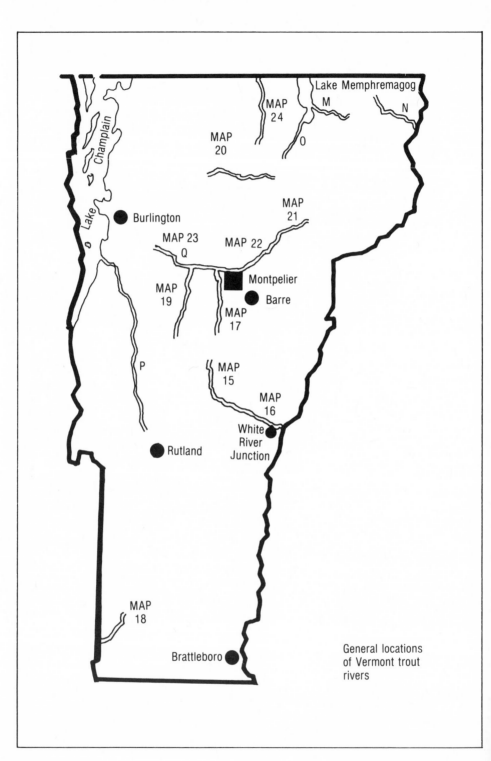

General locations
of Vermont trout
rivers

Chapter 5
The Rivers of Vermont

The first time I fished in Vermont was in 1979. I left my southern Maine home early one morning, arriving on the banks of the famed Battenkill River south of Manchester in time for some afternoon and evening fishing.

I had heard and read much about this legendary trout stream. The pages of fishing magazines and books are filled with stories of the big browns, rich insect life, and challenges that the Battenkill has to offer. Needless to say, I was not disappointed — the Battenkill was everything (and more) that I had hoped for. I managed to entice too few trout to a number 16 Henryville Special during a light brown caddis fly hatch. But from that day on, I have been a Battenkill addict — annual trips are planned. Unfortunately, not all of them pan out, and I am forced to rely on memory to explain how magnificent this trout stream really is.

In fact, "magnificent" is the word I'd use to sum up all the trout streams of Vermont. Whether it be the Battenkill, the White, the Mad, the Dog, the Winooski, the Lamoille — or one of the many other trout streams and rivers the state has to offer the fly fisherman, there is no other way to describe them. Each provides the *challenges* every fly fisherman is looking for in a trout stream. And each provides the *interesting* qualities which make a stream a joy to fish. But each is different — special in its own right.

The White River, for example, was a joy to me personally. I enjoy fishing riffle stretches and moderate rapids — with which the White is blessed. The Mad River, on the other hand, with its slow-moving stretches, presented its own interesting challenges; and so did all the others. Vermont is the place for fly fishermen with varied interests — they will not be disappointed.

Of course, fly fishing in Vermont is much, much more than simply catching trout; it is an experience, one you will not soon forget. The countryside through which Vermont's major trout streams flow is among the most scenic in New England. The air is fresh and clean; the water is pure; the people are friendly. Most rivers and streams are bordered with hardwoods and/or agricultural lands, and access to most of them is easy; knocking on the door of a farmhouse and politely asking for permission will nearly always gain access to a hidden stretch of river.

It is these things — the beauty of Vermont, the people, the easy way of life — that draw me to that state. The trout fishing there is some of the best in northern New England. But these other assets don't hurt a bit, and make Vermont (and fishing there) quite unique.

Like Maine and New Hampshire, the "native" trout of Vermont is the brook trout. In years past, the squaretail inhabited just about every stream and river that now contains browns or rainbow trout — but today, the better brook trout fishing is found in the higher elevations in the headwater sections. The brookie is still the most popular species with resident anglers, however.

Brown trout and rainbow trout are stocked heavily in Vermont and constitute much of the fishery in lower elevations and in the larger streams and rivers. These species grow to respectable weights (up to four and five pounds in some waters), and 11 to 14 inches is the average length.

The rivers and streams of Vermont flow outward from the center of the state. This region is mountainous, with some peaks reaching altitudes over 4,000 feet (many reach up over 3,000 feet). While water levels are greatly influenced by rain and snow-melt, most streams and rivers in the higher elevations remain relatively cool (in the mid- to-high 60s) throughout much of the fishing season. Stretches in the lower valleys may reach warmer temperatures. But being fed by upstream springs and mountain brooks, water temperatures do not suffer like those in Maine, in sections of New Hampshire, and in Massachusetts. Fishing is often surprisingly productive right through July and August.

From mid-May to mid-July is the prime fishing time in Vermont, however. Spring comes late to the mountains of Vermont — rivers and streams are apt to remain swollen until early May. Insect hatches start to appear about then, with dominant species emerging on through June.

Sporadic hatches continue later when conditions are right, offering dry fly action throughout the season. A small wet fly or a well-offered nymph will produce results during non-hatch periods, however.

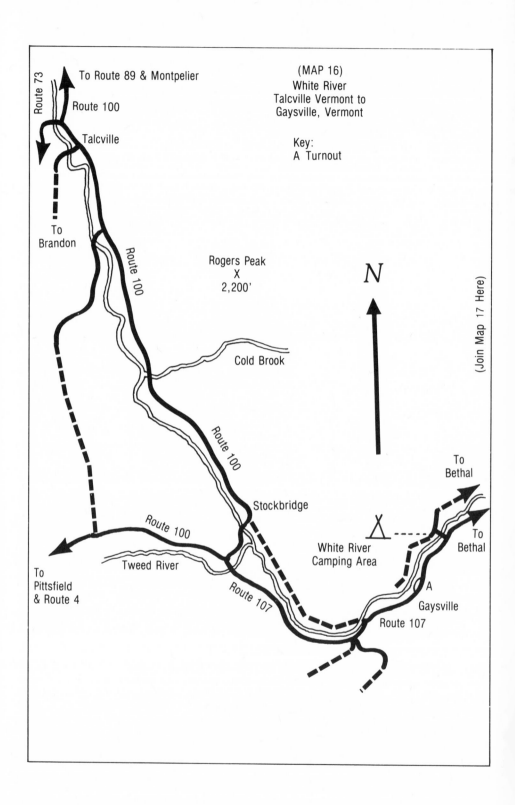

(MAP 16)
White River
Talcville Vermont to
Gaysville, Vermont

Key:
A Turnout

THE WHITE RIVER

Talcville to Gaysville

GENERAL DESCRIPTION

The White River from Talcville, downstream to Gaysville, (a distance of approximately 16 miles) is one of my favorite places in Vermont. It offers those slow-moving stretches and riffle sections so inviting to the trout fisherman. For the most part, brown trout and rainbow trout are the most available species, although scattered brook trout are taken on occasion.

From Talcville downstream to where the Tweed River enters the White River is generally a slow to moderate flow. It is broken by an occasional riffle or rapid stretch. The river swings away from Route 100, and excellent fishing is available. Access to many of these hidden sections may be obtained simply by stopping at a farmhouse and asking permission to fish the river.

From its confluence with the Tweed River downstream, the White River provides more fast-moving water. This is generally the case all the way to South Royalton. These riffles and rapids are the best spots to raise rainbow trout, while the pools generally provide the best brown trout action. The river is 40 to 50 feet wide in this section; it can be easily waded, although casting from the banks or from rocks is also possible. There are many long, deep, and amazingly clear pools which provide some most interesting and rewarding opportunities.

BEST PLACES TO FISH

The White River from Talcville downstream to somewhat below the White River Camping Area on Route 107 in Gaysville is worth fishing at nearly any point. Access is easy to most of this stretch, but permission to cross private lands should be obtained to reach sections running away from highways.

BEST TIMES TO FISH

Mid-May through June and into July is good. August can also be pro-

ductive in the faster areas and deeper pools, particularly early in the morning or in the late afternoon and evening hours. September and October are good months with subsurface flies, although the weather can be uncooperative at times.

BEST FLIES

Wet flies and streamers: Muddler, March Brown, Hare's Ear, Hendrickson, Dark Cahill, Blue Dun, Leadwing Coachman, Picket Pin, Quill Gordon, Stone Fly, and Female Beaverkill (sizes 10 to 14).

Nymphs: Hare's Ear, Otter Nymph, Muskrat Nymph, Atherton Dark, Hendrickson, March Brown, Black Stone, Brown Stone, Brown Caddis Pupa, Bird's Stone Fly No. 2, Black Nymph, Quill Gordon Nymph, and Gray Nymph (sizes 10 to 16).

Dry flies: Adams, March Brown, Hendrickson, Light Cahill, Cream Variant, Female Beaverkill, Hare's Ear, Pale Evening Dun, Whirling Blue Dun, Red Quill, Iron Blue Dun, Gray Fox, Hairwing Caddis, and Henryville Special (sizes 12 to 16).

GENERAL NOTES

The White River opens to fishing for all species of trout the second

Saturday in April. It closes the last Sunday in October. There is no minimum length limit, and there is a daily limit of 12 fish or five pounds. Camping facilities for those fishing this section are available at White River Campground in Gaysville. Write White River Valley Campground, Rt. 107, Gaysville, Vermont 05746; or telephone (802) 234-9115.

HOW TO REACH THE WHITE RIVER

From White River Junction, Vermont, take Route 89 north to Royalton, then take Route 107 west to Gaysville. Route 107 parallels the river in many places, and Route 100 travels north along the White River to Talcville.

From Rutland, Vermont, take Route 4 east to Route 100, then take Route 100 north to the junction with Route 107 west of Gaysville.

From Montpelier, Vermont, take Route 89 south to Royalton, then take Route 107 west to Gaysville.

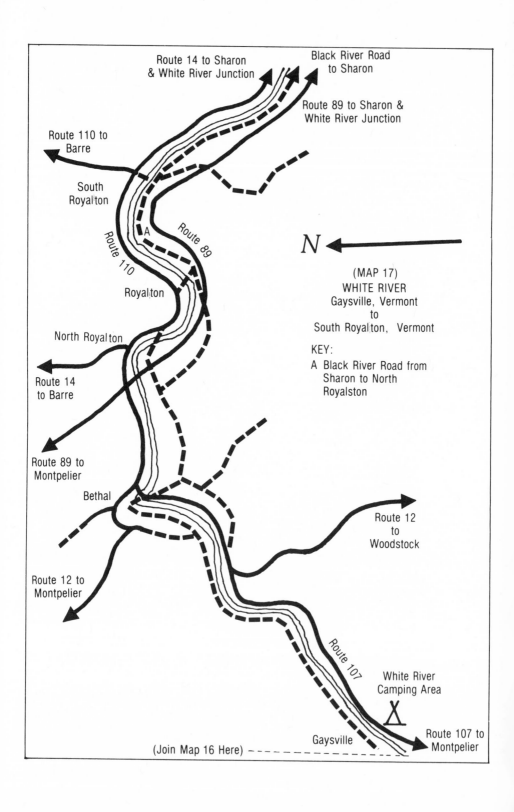

Route 14 to Sharon & White River Junction

Black River Road to Sharon

Route 89 to Sharon & White River Junction

Route 110 to Barre

South Royalton

Route 110

A

Route 89

Royalton

North Royalton

Route 14 to Barre

Route 89 to Montpelier

Bethal

Route 12 to Montpelier

N

(MAP 17)
WHITE RIVER
Gaysville, Vermont
to
South Royalton, Vermont

KEY:

A Black River Road from Sharon to North Royalston

Route 12 to Woodstock

Route 107

White River Camping Area

Gaysville

(Join Map 16 Here) ----

Route 107 to Montpelier

THE WHITE RIVER

Gaysville to South Royalton

GENERAL DESCRIPTION

From Gaysville downstream to the town of Bethel, the White River continues with a moderate rate of flow, providing riffles, rapids, and a host of deep pools to the fly fisherman. The best access points are along Route 107 west of Bethel, or from a rural road that parallels the river eastward after crossing the river at White River Campground. This road travels along the river all the way to Bethel, connecting with Route 12 there.

From Bethel downstream, the river widens and deepens. It continues to provide riffles and rapid stretches in some areas, but slow-moving current is dominant. Fishing for rainbow and brown trout remains better than average, however, particularly in the faster-moving runs, and where the riffles and rapids empty into pools.

BEST PLACES TO FISH

From Gaysville downstream to Bethel along Route 107, or off the dirt road on the river's north bank between Gaysville and Bethel.

From Royalton downstream to South Royalton off the Black River Road; fishermen will have to pick their way along, but the river comes within sight of this road in several places.

BEST TIMES TO FISH

Early May through June into mid-July is good; also, September and October to the end of the season.

BEST FLIES

Streamers and wet flies: Muddler, March Brown, Hare's Ear, Black Ghost, Hendrickson, Dark Cahill, Leadwing Coachman, and Picket Pin (sizes 8 to 12).

Nymphs: Hare's Ear, Otter Nymph, Muskrat Nymph, Brown Stone,

Bird's Stone Fly No. 2, Black Nymph, Gray Nymph, and March Brown (sizes 8 to 16).

Dry flies: Henryville Special, Downwing Caddis, Bucktail Caddis, Adams, Hendrickson, March Brown, Gray Fox, and Light Cahill (sizes 12 to 16).

GENERAL NOTES

This section of the White River opens at the same time as its upper section, the second Saturday in April, closing to fishing the last Sunday in October. The daily bag limit is also the same, 12 fish or five pounds.

HOW TO REACH THE WHITE RIVER (LOWER SECTION)

From White River Junction, Vermont, take Route 89 north to Royalton, then take Route 107 west to Gaysville, fishing the river along the way. You may continue on and cross the river at White River Campground and fish the river from the north bank downstream to Bethel.

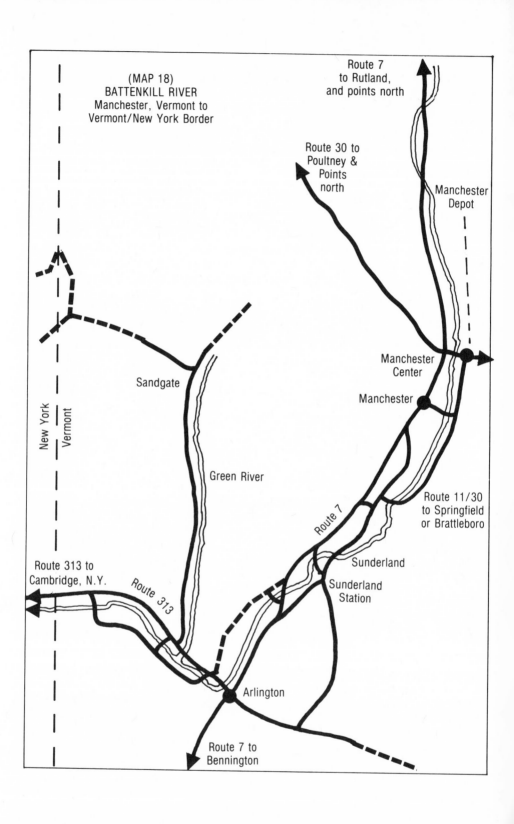

(MAP 18)
BATTENKILL RIVER
Manchester, Vermont to
Vermont/New York Border

Route 7
to Rutland,
and points north

Route 30 to
Poultney &
Points
north

Manchester
Depot

Manchester
Center

Manchester

New York | Vermont

Sandgate

Green River

Route 7

Route 11/30
to Springfield
or Brattleboro

Route 313 to
Cambridge, N.Y.

Route 313

Sunderland

Sunderland
Station

Arlington

Route 7 to
Bennington

THE BATTENKILL RIVER

Manchester to Vermont/New York Border

GENERAL DESCRIPTION

The Battenkill — oh, the Battenkill!! What can anyone say about this most renowned of New England's trout rivers? So much has been written describing the whims and secrets of this classic flowage that virtually every person in the Northeast who has ever picked up a fly rod has heard its name and the stories about the river's reluctant inhabitants.

The source of the Battenkill is Emerald Lake, which lies in the center of Emerald Lake State Park in Dorset, Vermont. It journeys southward at a rapid pace along Route 7, passing through East Dorset on its way to Manchester. This section is one of the best brook trout stretches on the river, although squaretails will be found all the way to the New York border.

Below Manchester, the Battenkill starts to form some of the pools and riffles for which it is so renowned. It continues on its southward course, traveling through the small hamlet of Sunderland. The town of Arlington is traversed next, within whose limits the Battenkill turns westward along Route 313, finally entering New York State.

The Battenkill is one of the finest natural brown trout streams in the Northeast. Excellent fishing for this species will be found just about everywhere from Manchester downstream to the New York border. Like most other Vermont rivers and streams, however, brook trout were at one time the principal fishery and the Battenkill continues to provide some magnificent native squaretail opportunities.

Catching fish on the Battenkill is no easy task. Brown trout exceeding five pounds exist in this river — fish of such weights cannot be considered easy prey. To raise the Battenkill fish, one must wade carefully and present, expertly and with a long leader, an exact imitation of the natural "fly of the moment" upon which the fish are feeding. To say that trout fishing on the Battenkill is some of the most challenging in the Northeast is putting it mildly. But I have to add that the Battenkill is a must for any serious fly fisherman. And once you fish there, it will not soon be forgotten — even if you came away shaking your head and empty-creeled.

BEST PLACES TO FISH

Excellent trout fishing will be found anywhere along the Battenkill. Some of the finest brook trout water is located upstream from Arlington. The brown trout enthusiast should concentrate on that section of river from Manchester to the New York border.

BEST TIMES TO FISH

The Battenkill is apt to produce action anytime throughout the Vermont open water fishing season. The most active fishing, however, starts in early May (around the 10th) when the first May fly hatches appear. May fly and caddis fly activity continues through the spring and summer, always emerging at specific times of the day and often in specific stretches of the river.

Water levels undergo their usual seasonal changes, reaching low levels as summer progresses. In upstream waters, tributaries from the mountains and springs keep water temperatures relatively cool, however — seldom do water temperatures exceed 70°. Midges and terrestrials entice fish to feed when hatches are not in progress, making the Battenkill a highly worthwhile river to visit and fish at any time during the season.

BEST FLIES

The insect life along the Battenkill is well-defined, and the best action is received by fishermen who know the river, know when a certain species is apt to appear and can match the natural and present an artificial expertly. When trout are selective (which is much of the time), 5-6X tippets and flies tied on #16 to #20 hooks are needed.

The following fly patterns are apt to produce action at specific times of the season: Muddler, Spuddler (spring and non-emerging periods), sizes 10-12; Quill Gordon, sizes 12 to 14; March Brown, sizes 12 to 14; Gray Fox, size 12; Dark Brown Hendrickson Nymph, size 12; Red Quill, size 14; Hendrickson, sizes 12 to 14; Mahogany Dun, size 16; Henryville Special, sizes 12 to 16; Paradrake, size 10; Olive Ephemerella, sizes 16 to 18; Blue-Wing Olive Dun, size 16; Hairwing Caddis, sizes 14 to 16; and Black Ant, sizes 14 to 20.

GENERAL NOTES

The Battenkill River opens to fishing the second Saturday of April; it closes the last Saturday in October.

Campgrounds are available in Arlington and at Emerald Lake State

Park. Lodging is availabe at inns and motels in Manchester and Arlington, and along Routes 7 and 313.

HOW TO REACH THE BATTENKILL RIVER

From Boston, take the Concord Turnpike to Acton, then take Route 2 west to North Adams. From North Adams, take Route 7 north to Arlington, Vermont.

From Concord, New Hampshire, take Route 9 west through Keene, New Hampshire and Brattleboro, Vermont to Bennington, Vermont, then go north on Route 7 to Arlington.

From Portland, Maine, take the Maine Turnpike south to Kittery, then follow Interstate 95 south to Interstate 495 at Amesbury, Massachusetts. Follow 495 to Littleton, then take Route 2 west through Leominster and Millers Falls to North Adams. Take Route 7 from North Adams to Arlington.

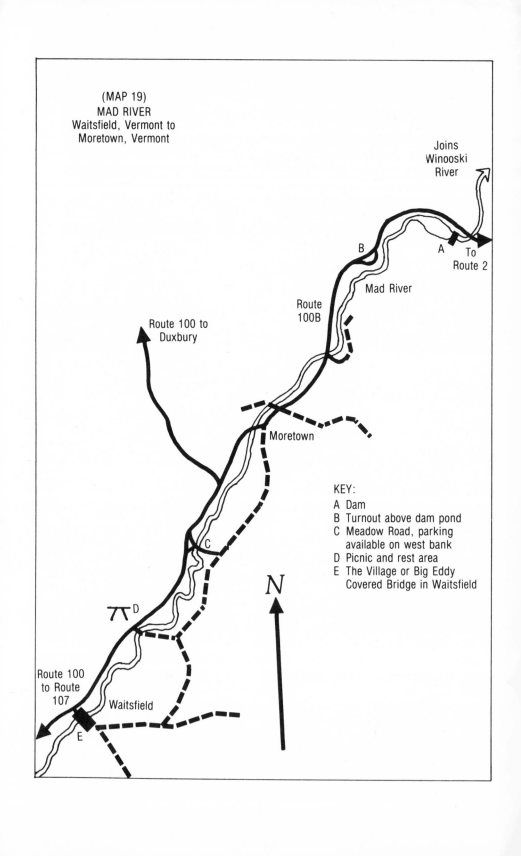

(MAP 19)
MAD RIVER
Waitsfield, Vermont to
Moretown, Vermont

Joins
Winooski
River

B

A To
Route 2

Mad River

Route
100B

Route 100 to
Duxbury

Moretown

KEY:
A Dam
B Turnout above dam pond
C Meadow Road, parking
available on west bank
D Picnic and rest area
E The Village or Big Eddy
Covered Bridge in Waitsfield

C

N

D

Route 100
to Route
107

Waitsfield

E

THE MAD RIVER

Waitsfield to Moretown

GENERAL DESCRIPTION

The Mad River is a nice little trout stream, flowing generally northward from the Green Mountain National Forest in Warren, to the Winooski River at Moretown. Its upper stretches are nothing more than a mountainous trickle containing populations of native brook trout; it is not until the Mad River leaves its mountain source and enters the town of Waitsfield that it is fishable.

From this point downstream, the Mad twists and turns past wooded and agricultural lands, forming some interesting pools and moderate riffles. The river is stocked with rainbow trout and brown trout, and good fishing is available for both species.

Originating in the Green Mountains, the Mad River is influenced by small tributaries and springs. While it may reach low levels during mid-summer, water temperatures are maintained at relatively cool levels throughout the fishing season. Fishing can be good at any time. Access is relatively easy, since the river parallels major highways for much of its length. Some sections do meander away from roads, however, but the fisherman will have no difficulty finding a place to wet his line.

Below Moretown, the character of this river changes. It is slower, but riffles are found at several places. Fishing is good all the way to the dead-water formed by a dam upstream from the Winooski River.

BEST PLACES TO FISH

For rainbow trout, the riffle areas in Waitsfield and Moretown are good. For brown trout, the slower stretches and riffle sections in these two towns should be considered. The fisherman should not overlook the deeper pools, undercut banks, and boulders and logs along the banks. All are potential holding spots.

Three notable stretches are: at the picnic area and rest stop on Route 100 in Waitsfield; where the river passes under the Meadow Road in Waitsfield; and upstream from the turnouts on Route 100B below the village of Moretown.

BEST TIMES TO FISH

Early May with small wet flies and dry flies as insect hatches appear, through June. July can be a worthwhile period early in the mornings and in the afternoon and evening hours with dry flies during sporadic insect hatches. September and October can be productive with small wet flies, terrestrial imitations, and small streamers.

BEST FLIES

Wet flies: Light Cahill, Dark Cahill, Muddler, Hendrickson, March Brown, Stone Fly, Ginger Quill, Female Beaverkill, Coachman, Iron Blue Dun, and Gold-Ribbed Hare's Ear (sizes 10 to 14).

Dry flies: Adams, March Brown, Light Cahill, Dark Cahill, Hare's Ear, Pale Evening Dun, Whirling Blue Dun, Quill Gordon, Gray Fox, Iron Blue Dun, Hairwing Caddis, and Henryville Special (sizes 12 to 14).

Nymphs: Gray Fox Nymph, Zug Bug, Iron Blue Nymph, Light Cahill Nymph, Leadwing Coachman Nymph, Hendrickson Nymph, Black Stone, and Brown Caddis Pupa (sizes 10 to 16).

GENERAL NOTES

The Mad River opens to fishing the second Saturday in April. It closes the last Sunday in October. There is a 12-fish or five-pound daily limit.

HOW TO REACH THE MAD RIVER

From Concord, New Hampshire, take Route 89 to Montpelier, Vermont, then go south on Route 100B to Moretown and Waitsfield.

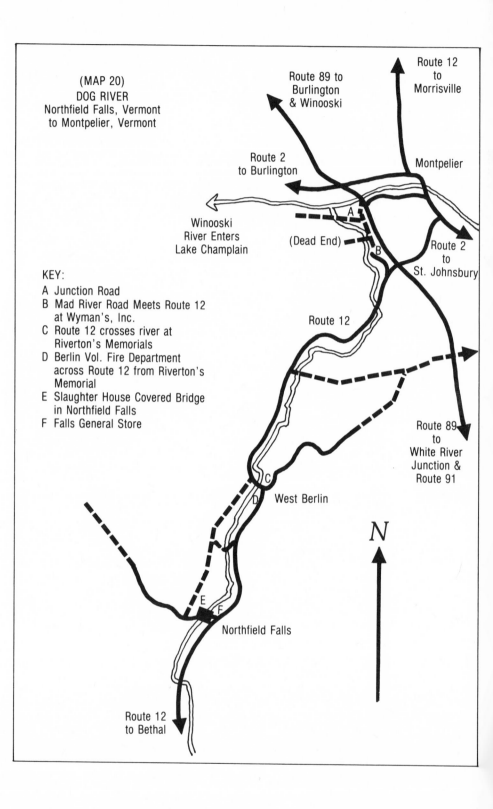

(MAP 20)
DOG RIVER
Northfield Falls, Vermont
to Montpelier, Vermont

Route 89 to
Burlington
& Winooski

Route 12
to
Morrisville

Route 2
to Burlington

Montpelier

Winooski
River Enters
Lake Champlain

A

(Dead End)

B

Route 2
to
St. Johnsbury

KEY:

A Junction Road
B Mad River Road Meets Route 12
   at Wyman's, Inc.
C Route 12 crosses river at
   Riverton's Memorials
D Berlin Vol. Fire Department
   across Route 12 from Riverton's
   Memorial
E Slaughter House Covered Bridge
   in Northfield Falls
F Falls General Store

Route 12

Route 89
to
White River
Junction &
Route 91

C

D West Berlin

N

E
F

Northfield Falls

Route 12
to Bethal

THE DOG RIVER

Northfield Falls to Montpelier

GENERAL DESCRIPTION

The Dog River is another of those small, central Vermont streams containing good populations of trout. While the Dog River is not as esthetically rewarding, or as consistent throughout the season, as the Mad River, it is a river to fish if you happen to be in the Montpelier area. To be honest, however, the Dog is *not* worth a special fishing trip to Vermont, although good fishing for rainbow trout and brown trout is available at specific times.

Having its source in the hill country of Roxbury, the Dog River, like the Mad River, flows northward, joining the Winooski River at Montpelier. Its upper reaches house brook trout, while its middle and lower stretches are stocked with browns and rainbows. Overall, the Dog is quite narrow until it enters the town of Northfield Falls, at which point it widens a bit. It is the stretch from Northfield Falls downstream to Montpelier where the fisherman should concentrate efforts. Some limited success with brown trout may also be found upstream to about the Roxbury town line, in selected places.

From Northfield Falls to the city limits of Montpelier, the Dog River travels through mixed terrain of woodlands and agricultural lands. Its drop is moderate but not overwhelming, providing a consistent current, short riffles, some deep pools, and other challenging characteristics of a small river. The river is narrow for much of its length, and is well-bordered by mature tree growth and bushes in many places, requiring from the fisherman slow, careful, patient wading and well-executed casts and presentations to all possible holding areas. If a fisherman takes his time, fishing carefully, diligently, and patiently, good results are possible.

BEST PLACES TO FISH

Approximately one mile north of Northfield Falls, a dirt road leaves Route 12 on the left, crossing the Central Vermont Railroad tracks.

About 100 yards further, a bridge crosses the river. This bridge is the best place to start fishing the river. A set of riffles and deep pools will be found just below the bridge, while quiet water will be seen upstream. The fisherman can work in either direction and find results on both brown trout and rainbow trout.

At the hamlet of West Berlin, the river passes under Route 12. There is a good set of riffles and moderate current here; wet flies do well. Continuing downstream, the river comes within sight of Route 12 in several places and passes under a couple of unnamed dirt roads leading to the right; these sections should all be considered. This is primarily brown trout water all the way to the Winooski confluence.

Another access point and section worth considering lies off the Dog River Road in Montpelier. This road leads left off Route 12 just before Wyman's, Inc. and travels to the Montpelier Recreational Field. One-half mile further, a gated dirt road crosses the river to the left. The Dog River Road continues and meets the Junction Road, which also crosses the river just before it enters the Winooski River. All these sections are worth trying.

BEST TIMES TO FISH

Early May with small wet flies and small streamers, through June (and much of July) with subsurface flies except during hatch periods. August can produce limited action in the deep pools and riffle areas. September and October can offer some action with subsurface flies and terrestrial imitations.

BEST FLIES

Streamers and wet flies: Muddler, Spuddler, March Brown, Hendrickson, Light Cahill, Quill Gordon, Stone Fly, Hare's Ear, Blue Dun, and Coachman (sizes 10 to 14).

Dry Flies: Adams, March Brown, Light Cahill, Cream Variant, Hare's Ear, Quill Gordon, Gray Fox, Iron Blue Dun, Downwing Caddis, and Henryville Special (sizes 12 to 14).

GENERAL NOTES

The Dog River opens to fishing the second Saturday in April, closing the last Sunday in October. The daily bag limit is 12 fish or five pounds.

Lodging facilities are available at motels in Montpelier.

HOW TO REACH THE DOG RIVER

From Concord, New Hampshire, take Route 89 to Montpelier, Vermont, then follow Route 12 along the river as far as Northfield Falls.

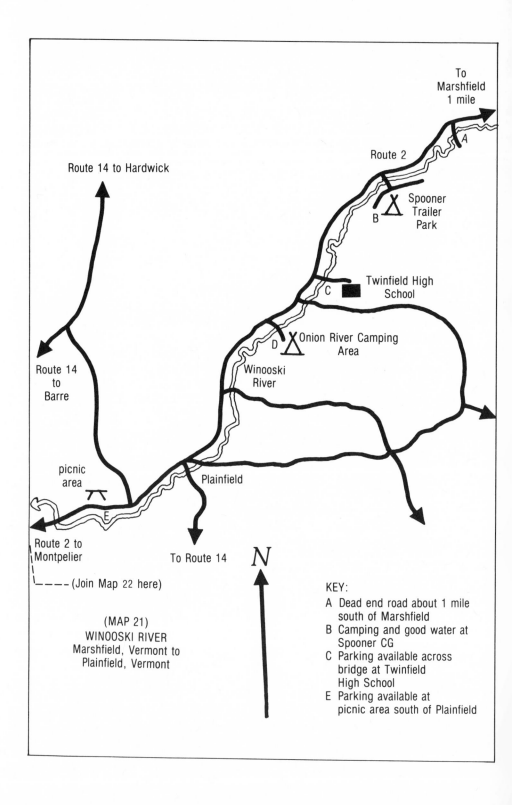

To
Marshfield
1 mile

A

Route 2

Spooner
Trailer
Park

B

C Twinfield High
School

Route 14 to Hardwick

Route 14
to
Barre

D Onion River Camping
Area

Winooski
River

picnic
area

Plainfield

E

Route 2 to
Montpelier

To Route 14

N

(Join Map 22 here)

(MAP 21)
WINOOSKI RIVER
Marshfield, Vermont to
Plainfield, Vermont

KEY:
A Dead end road about 1 mile
  south of Marshfield
B Camping and good water at
  Spooner CG
C Parking available across
  bridge at Twinfield
  High School
E Parking available at
  picnic area south of Plainfield

THE WINOOSKI RIVER
Marshfield to Plainfield

GENERAL DESCRIPTION

There are several rivers in Vermont which are acclaimed for their trout fisheries and for what they have to offer the trout enthusiasts; the Winooski River is one of those rivers. While the Winooski cannot keep step with the Battenkill, it does nevertheless offer some of the finest brown trout and rainbow trout fishing to be found in central Vermont.

To put it plainly, the upper Winooski is a river for fly fishermen of all interests and degrees of skill. More, it is one of those rivers that is a pleasure to explore and fish. The countryside through which it flows is rural (except for small hamlets), surrounded by rolling Vermont hills, thick forests, and agricultural lands. The Winooski ranks high on my list of Vermont trout streams, not only because of the potential I know is there, but also because of all the qualities which make the Winooski a unique stream.

The Winooski is formed by several small tributaries in the rolling hill country of Cabot. Its uppermost section, from north of Lower Cabot to Marshfield, is a narrow, fast-flowing trickle containing populations of brook trout and rainbow trout. As might be expected, the water is clear and, coming from the highlands, much of the river — as far downstream as Plainfield and East Montpelier — is kept at cool temperatures throughout the fishing season.

Below Marshfield, the Winooski's rate of flow slows somewhat. It widens slightly, and twists and turns, forming some interesting pools, separated by riffles and small rapid stretches. For the most part, this secton is inhabited by brown trout, although rainbow trout may be discovered as you travel downstream towards Plainfield. The river is not overly wide, requiring short, well-delivered and well-placed casts to prospective holding areas, which are virtually behind every rock, boulder, or log, and beneath every undercut bank.

BEST PLACES TO FISH

Excellent fishing will be found just about anywhere on the Winooski from Marshfield to Plainfield. The river comes within sight of Route 2 in many places — these spots should be examined carefully. Better success will be found if the fisherman takes the time to work upstream or downstream from these easily accessible areas, however, since they are the hardest hit.

Also, several dirt roads lead off Route 2 to the right (going north) and cross the river. Most are not marked, requiring the fisherman to explore. He will not have to travel far, however, since the river is not a great distance from Route 2.

BEST TIMES TO FISH

Spring comes late to the Winooski River valley. Snowmelt is still taking place into late April or early May in the hidden valleys — so water levels in the Winooski remain high, almost at unfishable levels until the middle of May. Early action is possible with streamers and bucktails, but conditions are far from ideal.

Generally, water levels start to recede to fishable levels around the 10th or 15th of May, reaching normal flow by the end of the month. June is excellent. July continues to produce good catches except during the heat of the day; mornings and mid-afternoons to dusk are the best.

This upper section of the Winooski may be considered low by many fishermen in August, but limited action is possible in the riffle stretches and deeper pools. Generally, however, the river is not fished a great deal from mid-July until mid-September, when action resumes and continues through October to the end of the season.

BEST FLIES

Streamers and wet flies: Muddler, Spuddler, March Brown, Light Cahill, Hendrickson, Quill Gordon, Stone Fly, Coachman, Hare's Ear, Picket Pin, Leadwing Coachman, Blue Dun, and Hendrickson Emerger (sizes 10 to 14). These will produce well anytime, except during insect hatches.

Dry flies: Adams, March Brown, Red Quill, Hendrickson, Mosquito, Light Cahill, Grey Fox, Green Drake, Blue-Wing Olive, Henryville Special, and Hairwing Caddis (sizes 12 to 16).

GENERAL NOTES

The Winooski River opens to fishing the second Saturday in April and closes the last Saturday in October. The daily creel limit is 12 fish or five pounds.

Camping facilities along this upper section of the Winooski are conveniently located at Onion River Camping Area, located off Route 2 north of Plainfield. Another camping area, Spooner Trailer Park, is located one and one-half miles further, just over the Marshfield town line.

HOW TO REACH THE UPPER WINOOSKI RIVER

From greater Boston, take Route 93 north to Manchester and Concord, New Hampshire. From Concord, take Route 89 to Montpelier, Vermont, then go east on Route 2 to Plainfield and Marshfield.

From Portland, Maine, take the Maine Turnpike south to Kittery, then follow Interstate 95 south to Interstate 495 in Massachusetts. Take Interstate 495 to Route 213, follow Route 213 to Methuen then go north on Route 93 to Concord, New Hampshire. At Concord take Route 89 to Montpelier, Vermont, then go east on Route 2 to Plainfield and Marshfield.

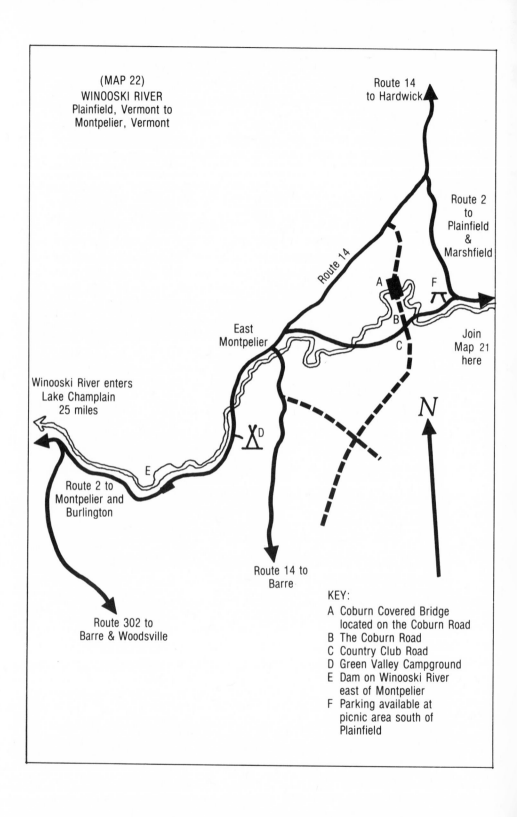

(MAP 22)
WINOOSKI RIVER
Plainfield, Vermont to
Montpelier, Vermont

Route 14
to Hardwick

Route 2
to
Plainfield
&
Marshfield

Route 14

A
F
B
C

Join
Map 21
here

East
Montpelier

Winooski River enters
Lake Champlain
25 miles

N

D

E

Route 2 to
Montpelier and
Burlington

Route 14 to
Barre

Route 302 to
Barre & Woodsville

KEY:
A Coburn Covered Bridge
  located on the Coburn Road
B The Coburn Road
C Country Club Road
D Green Valley Campground
E Dam on Winooski River
  east of Montpelier
F Parking available at
  picnic area south of
  Plainfield

THE WINOOSKI RIVER

Plainfield to Montpelier

GENERAL DESCRIPTION

From Plainfield downstream to East Montpelier, the Winooski River displays the same characteristics as the section downstream from Marshfield — riffle stretches, deep pools, undercut banks, shallow spots and long, twisting slower sections. A noticeable difference, however, is that the river widens, taking on the assets of a growing river. It can be easily waded in most places, although the bottom is generally freestone and care should be taken.

Access to the Winooski River south of Plainfield is not overly difficult. Route 2 parallels the river in several places and while the river meanders away from the highway, several roads offer access by vehicle. One such spot is at the picnic area just south of Plainfield and the Coburn Road, which leads off Route 2 on the East Montpelier/Plainfield town line. This is a dirt road leading to a quiet stretch of river. Parking is limited, and landowners allow use of their land providing their rights are respected. Do not block gates leading into pastures, park as far off the road as possible, and, above all, *do not litter!*

From East Montpelier to the dam blocking the river east of Montpelier, the fisherman will find some most interesting water — riffles, rapids, and shaded banks. This is prime rainbow trout water, although brown trout are available as well.

BEST PLACES TO FISH

At the picnic area on Route 2 south of Plainfield (including those areas just upstream and downstream). Fishermen wading this section will find interesting possibilities away from the road.

Off the Coburn Road in East Montpelier is generally slow-moving water mixed with riffles. Good May fly and caddis fly hatches in late May and June.

Also try along Route 2 from the dam in Montpelier to East Montpelier.

BEST TIMES TO FISH

Mid- to late May through June into mid- or late July. August in the mornings and late afternoons to dusk. September and October.

BEST FLIES

Those flies recommended under that section of the Winooski River from Marshfield to Plainfield are good patterns from Plainfield to Montpelier.

GENERAL NOTES

The Winooski opens to fishing the second Saturday in April, closing the last Sunday in October. The daily creel limit is 12 fish or five pounds.

Camping facilities are available at Green Valley Campground, located on Route 2 west of East Montpelier. Hotels and motels will also be found in Montpelier.

HOW TO REACH THE WINOOSKI RIVER

From greater Boston, take Route 93 north to Manchester and Concord,

New Hampshire. From Concord take Route 89 to Montpelier, Vermont, then go east on Route 2.

From Portland, Maine, take the Maine Turnpike south to Kittery, then take Interstate 95 south to Interstate 495 in Massachusetts. Take Interstate 495 to Route 213, follow Route 213 to Methuen, then go north on Route 93 to Concord, New Hampshire. At Concord, take Route 89 to Montpelier, then go east on Route 2.

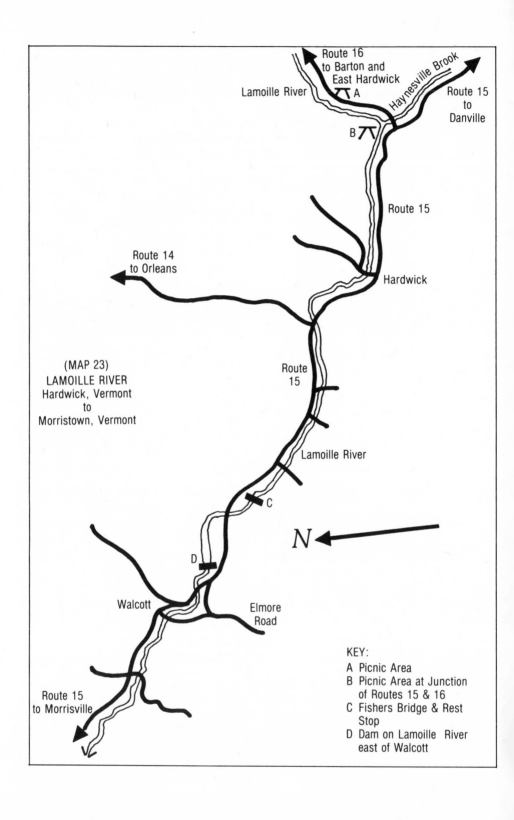

Route 16
to Barton and
East Hardwick

Haynesville Brook

Lamoille River

A

Route 15
to
Danville

B

Route 15

Route 14
to Orleans

Hardwick

(MAP 23)
LAMOILLE RIVER
Hardwick, Vermont
to
Morristown, Vermont

Route
15

Lamoille River

C

N

Walcott

Elmore
Road

Route 15
to Morrisville

KEY:
A Picnic Area
B Picnic Area at Junction
  of Routes 15 & 16
C Fishers Bridge & Rest
  Stop
D Dam on Lamoille River
  east of Walcott

D

THE LAMOILLE RIVER

Hardwick to Morrisville

GENERAL DESCRIPTION

Other than the Battenkill and the Winooski, the Lamoille River from Hardwick to Morrisville is my favorite stretch of trout water in Vermont. I've fished it several times, and each time I find challenges, good fishing, and esthetic rewards on this pleasing river.

The Lamoille River has its own source in Horse Pond, situated alongside Route 16 in the rolling hills of Greensboro. It travels southward at a rapid, tumbling pace to Hardwick, where it turns due west. From its source to Greensboro Bend, the Lamoille is basically a brook trout stream — rainbow trout are available downstream to Hardwick; browns will also be found from East Hardwick to Hardwick.

Once leaving the town of Hardwick, the Lamoille travels alongside Route 15 to Walcott, then on to Morrisville, twisting away from the highway on occasion. The characteristics of the river in this section are a mixture of riffles and slow stretches, bordered by forests, brush growth, and cultivated fields. Rainbow trout are the principal species, although brown trout are also available (big ones, up to two and three pounds!).

The Lamoille is an interesting river. While it does experience good hatches of May flies and caddis flies, and while I have taken trout with popular dry fly and terrestrial imitations, it is basically a wet fly and small streamer fly river. During insect hatches when dry flies are expected to produce results, wet flies fished just under the surface, and emerging patterns, seem to offer the best action. This was interesting, and perplexing, to me the first time I fished the Lamoille and has always challenged me when fishing this river. It will undoubtedly intrigue and challenge you, too.

BEST PLACES TO FISH

From East Hardwick downstream along Route 16 and Route 15 to Hardwick.

From Hardwick downstream along Route 15 to Fisher's Bridge in Walcott. Slow water, broken by occasional riffles, characterize this section.

From Walcott Village downstream to the river's intersection with Route 15A in Morrisville. Several unnamed dirt roads lead off Route 15 in this section, crossing the river and offering access to areas traveling away from the highway.

BEST TIMES TO FISH

Mid-May through June and into Mid-July. September and October. In May and June, action is possible just about anytime during the day — mornings, early afternoons, and evenings are peak periods. As water levels recede and temperatures rise in July, fish later in the afternoon.

BEST FLIES

Wet flies and streamers: Muddler, Light Cahill, Ginger Quill, Quill Gordon, Dark Cahill, Female Beaverkill, Coachman, Hendrickson, Iron Blue Dun, Hare's Ear, March Brown, Blue Dun, and Leadwing Coachman (sizes 10 to 14).

Dry flies: Adams, March Brown, Light Cahill, Hendrickson, Red Quill, Quill Gordon, and Grey Fox (sizes 12 to 14).

GENERAL NOTES

The Lamoille River opens to fishing the second Saturday in April, closing the last Sunday in October. While there is a 12-fish or five-pound daily limit, *all* trout, including browns, rainbows, and brookies must be at least six inches in length from the waters of Caledonia and Lamoille counties; this section of the Lamoille River flows through both of these counties.

Lodging facilities along the Lamoille are available at Mountain View Cabins, located on Route 15 just east of Morrisville. Camping facilities are limited.

HOW TO REACH THE LAMOILLE RIVER

From greater Boston, take Route 93 north to Concord, New Hampshire, then take Route 89 north to Montpelier, Vermont. From Montpelier, take Route 12 north to Morrisville, then go east on Route 15 to Hardwick.

From Portland, Maine, take the Maine Turnpike south to Kittery, then Interstate 95 south to Interstate 495 in Massachusetts. Take Interstate 495 to Route 213, then follow Route 213 west to Methuen, then Route

93 north to Concord, New Hampshire. From Concord, take Route 89 to Montpelier, Vermont, then follow Route 12 north to Morrisville.

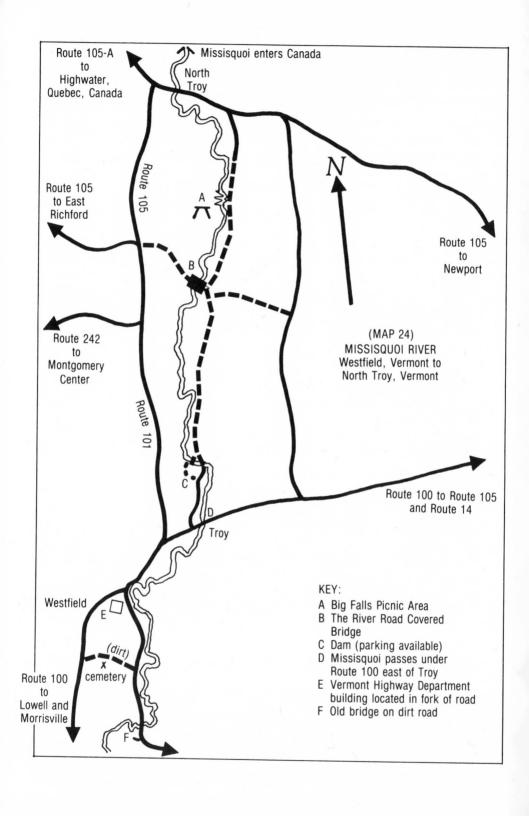

Route 105-A
to
Highwater,
Quebec, Canada

Missisquoi enters Canada

North
Troy

Route 105

A

Route 105
to East
Richford

B

N

Route 105
to
Newport

Route 242
to
Montgomery
Center

Route 101

(MAP 24)
MISSISQUOI RIVER
Westfield, Vermont to
North Troy, Vermont

C

Route 100 to Route 105
and Route 14

D

Troy

Westfield

E

(dirt)
x
cemetery

Route 100
to
Lowell and
Morrisville

F

KEY:
A Big Falls Picnic Area
B The River Road Covered
   Bridge
C Dam (parking available)
D Missisquoi passes under
   Route 100 east of Troy
E Vermont Highway Department
   building located in fork of road
F Old bridge on dirt road

THE MISSISQUOI RIVER

Westfield to North Troy

GENERAL DESCRIPTION

The upper stretch of the Missisquoi River, between the towns of Westfield and North Troy, is a pleasant trout river, flowing through farmlands, rolling hills, and woodlands. As it enters the town of Westfield on its northerly course, the river is a narrow, tumbling flowage offering riffles and pools of moderate depths. It soon slows to a more pleasurable pace, and deepens, twists, and turns on its way to Troy. The Missisquoi is a brown trout river.

East of Troy, the Missisquoi passes under Route 100. It is wider in this section, with steep banks in many sections making wading difficult. After tumbling over the dam on the River Road, however, the river can be waded easily in many places, and offers some magnificent riffles, short rapids, pools, and undercut banks, all housing brown trout (some good-sized ones, too!).

Once passing under the Troy/North Troy covered bridge, the Missisquoi continues on with the same basic character. Wherever it turns, it provides interesting pools and faster-moving riffles. One scenic attraction in this section is Big Falls, with a drop of approximately 50 feet straight down through a steep-walled rock gorge. This is an excellent place for a picnic or lunch while fishing this stretch of the Missisquoi north of Troy.

BEST PLACES TO FISH

From where the river passes under a bridge on a dirt road forking off from Route 100 in Westfield to the bridge on Route 100 in Troy.

From the dam located on the River Road in Troy to Big Falls.

BEST TIMES TO FISH

Late May (spring comes late to this region of Vermont) through June and July. September and October.

BEST FLIES

Wet flies and streamers: Muddler, Black Nose Dace, March Brown, Light Cahill, Stone Fly, Hendrickson, Coachman, Female Beaverkill, Quill Gordon, Iron Blue Dun, Hare's Ear, Picket Pin, Leadwing Coachman, Grey Hackle, and Hendrickson Emerger (sizes 10 to 14).

Dry flies: The Missisquoi experiences good May fly and caddis fly hatches from late May through early July. Sporadic hatches occur right through the fishing season, particularly in the riffle sections. The Adams, Hendrickson, March Brown, Light Cahill, Red Quill, Whirling Blue Dun, Gray Fox, Iron Blue Dun, Cream Variant, Blue-Wing Oliver, Henryville Special, and Hairwing Caddis (sizes 12 to 16) are recommended.

GENERAL NOTES

The Missisquoi River opens to fishing the second Saturday in April. It closes the last Sunday in October. General daily bag limits apply.

HOW TO REACH THE MISSISQUOI RIVER

From Montpelier, Vermont, take Route 12 north to Morrisville, then Route 100 north to Westfield. Note Map #23 for directions to access points and directions to River Road and Big Falls.

OTHER VERMONT RIVERS

THE CLYDE RIVER

GENERAL DESCRIPTION

The Clyde River is a tributary of Lake Memphremagog. It is not a large river, but offers limited salmon and trout fishing opportunities at specific times of the fishing season. Water reaches low levels by mid-summer in the upper reaches near West Charleston, but annual stocking of brown trout make it worth fishing if you happen to be in the area.

BEST PLACES TO FISH

For landlocked salmon: in the town of Newport upstream to the dam at Clyde Pond.

For brown trout: from Lubber Lake in West Charleston downstream to Lake Salem.

BEST TIMES TO FISH

For landlocked salmon: early April through mid-May, mid-September to end of fishing season.

For brown trout: mid-May through June, late September to end of fishing season.

BEST FLIES

For landlocked salmon: Gray Ghost, Black Ghost, Mickey Finn, and other streamers.

For brown trout: wet flies — March Brown, Light Cahill, Hendrickson, and other natural-colored sub-surface patterns (sizes 10 to 14).

GENERAL NOTES

The fishing season opens on the Clyde River for landlocked salmon and brown trout the second Saturday in April, closing on both species the last Sunday in October.

The daily creel limit on browns is 12 fish or 5 pounds. The daily creel limit on salmon is two, minimum length limit, 15 inches.

HOW TO REACH THE CLYDE RIVER

From Brattleboro, Vermont, and points south take Route 91 north to Newport.

NULHEGAN RIVER

GENERAL DESCRIPTION

The source of the Nulhegan River is Nulhegan Pond in Brighton. It travels eastward through the lowlands of Ferdinand and Brunswick, finally entering the Connecticut River at Bloomfield. The Nulhegan offers good brook trout fishing in its upper sections, although access is difficult to many sections. There are brown trout as you travel upstream from the Connecticut River.

BEST PLACES TO FISH

From the village of Bloomfield upstream along Route 105 to the Bloomfield/Brunswick town line.

BEST TIMES TO FISH

Mid-May through June into early July. September and October.

BEST FLIES

Wet flies: Hendrickson, Light Cahill, March Brown, and other natural-colored sub-surface imitations.

GENERAL NOTES

The Nulhegan opens to fishing the second Saturday in April, closing the last Sunday in October. General daily bag limits apply.

HOW TO REACH THE NULHEGAN RIVER

From St. Johnsbury, Vermont, take Route 91 north to Lyndonville, then take Route 114 north to its junction with Route 105. Go east on Route 105 to Bloomfield.

BLACK RIVER

GENERAL DESCRIPTION

The Black River is a tributary of Lake Memphremagog, entering that large body of water at South Bay in Newport. The Black is a productive trout river, containing both brown trout and rainbow trout from its source near Irasburg to its confluence with South Bay. This river experiences large runs of rainbow trout each spring in the vicinity of South Bay. This river should not be confused with the Black River in Ludlow, Vermont. The Black River described here is smaller, flowing through rich farmlands and rolling hills, but is nevertheless a fine trout stream. The river flows northward.

BEST PLACES TO FISH

Trout will be found from Irasburg downstream, but some of the finest opportunities will be discovered from the town of Coventry downstream along Route 5 to Lake Memphremagog. Fishermen should start at the covered bridge located on the Coventry Road, exploring sections along Route 5. Both riffles and moderately flowing stretches will be found. That stretch from Irasburg to Coventry, off the mouth of the Black River in South Bay, should not be neglected, however. Try this spot in the spring.

BEST FLIES

Wet flies: March Brown, Hendrickson, Light Cahill, Woolly Worm, Blue Dun, Grey Hackle, Hendrickson Emerger, Leadwing Coachman, Picket Pin, and other natural-colored sub-surface imitations (sizes 10 to 12).

BEST TIMES TO FISH

Early April for spawning rainbows at South Bay; mid-May through June into early July; September and October.

GENERAL NOTES

The Black River opens to fishing the second Saturday in April, closing to fishing the last Sunday in October. On that section of Black River from approximately Irasburg downstream to the Route 5 bridge in Coventry, the daily creel limit is two fish with a minimum length limit of 10 inches. The remainder of the river is governed by general law.

HOW TO REACH THE BLACK RIVER

From Montpelier, Vermont, take Route 14 north to Irasburg, then follow Route 5 north along the river. From White River Junction, Vermont, take Route 91 north to Orleans, then follow Route 58 west to Irasburg, then take Route 5 north along the Black River towards Newport.

OTTER CREEK

GENERAL DESCRIPTION

The longest stream solely within the State of Vermont is Otter Creek. Starting at Emerald Lake (the source also of the Battenkill), Otter Creek runs due north for nearly 90 miles, passing through such towns and cities as Danby, Wallingford, Rutland, Brandon, Middlebury, and Vergennes before emptying into Lake Champlain. Within the valley of Otter Creek is an assortment of water characteristics which make it one of Vermont's most important and popular fishing attractions.

The upper sections of the creek are known for native brook trout. This species will be found in good numbers from Emerald Lake downstream all the way to Rutland. While the average squaretail measures 8 to 12 inches in most sections, lunker trout have been taken, particularly in the back bogs that fishermen cannot easily reach. From Rutland to Brandon, brown trout take over, with limited populations available down to Middlebury.

BEST PLACES TO FISH

Unquestionably the best section of Otter Creek for the fly fisherman lies from Emerald Lake downstream through the towns of Mount Tabor, South Wallingford, Clarendon, and Alfrecha to the Rutland city limit. The upper section of the Battenkill, with the creek widening and forming inviting riffles and pools as it travels north. Route 7 parallels Otter Creek much of the way, with many town roads crossing the creek and offering excellent access points.

BEST TIMES TO FISH

Mid-May through June and into early July; September and October.

BEST FLIES

Wet flies and streamers: Muddler, March Brown, Hendrickson, Light Cahill, and other natural-colored sub-surface imitations. Terrestrial dry flies produce well in the pools and riffle sections as the season progresses, with the popular May fly and caddis fly patterns taking trout during periods of peak activity (from approximately late May through June).

GENERAL NOTES

Otter Creek opens to fishing the second Saturday in April, closing the last Sunday in October. Check Vermont Digest of Fish and Game Laws for any special regulations on certain sections.

Campground along Otter Creek are located at Emerald Lake State Park in Dorset, and along Route 7 in Wallingford. Picnic areas can also be found along Route 7.

HOW TO REACH OTTER CREEK

From greater Boston, take Route 93 to Manchester and Concord, New Hampshire, then take Route 89 to White River Junction, Vermont. Take Route 4 to Rutland then go south on Route 7 to Clarendon and Wallingford.

WINOOSKI RIVER

GENERAL DESCRIPTION

Once leaving Montpelier, the Winooski River widens and deepens to become a major Vermont river. It contains large brown and rainbow trout — excellent fishing is possible to the patient fly fisherman who takes the time to fish this section slowly. Because of the river's width and depth in many places, it cannot easily be waded, but casting from shore or other vantage points is possible.

BEST PLACES TO FISH

Good fishing is available just about anywhere from Montpelier to Jonesville.

BEST TIMES TO FISH

Mid-May through June; mid- to late September through October.

BEST FLIES

One of the most productive methods of catching the large browns and rainbows in this section of the Winooski is with live bait or lures. Fly fishermen should utilize casting streamers which imitate important forage fish on hook sizes ranging from #4 through #8.

GENERAL NOTES

The Winooski River opens to fishing the second Saturday in April, closing to fishing the last Sunday in October. Check the Vermont Digest of Fish and Game Laws for any existing special regulations.

HOW TO REACH THE WINOOSKI RIVER

From greater Boston, take Route 93 to Concord, New Hampshire, then Route 89 to Montpelier, Vermont. Take Route 2 west to Duxbury, then proceed to North Duxbury on the south side of the river or continue on to Bolton via Route 2.

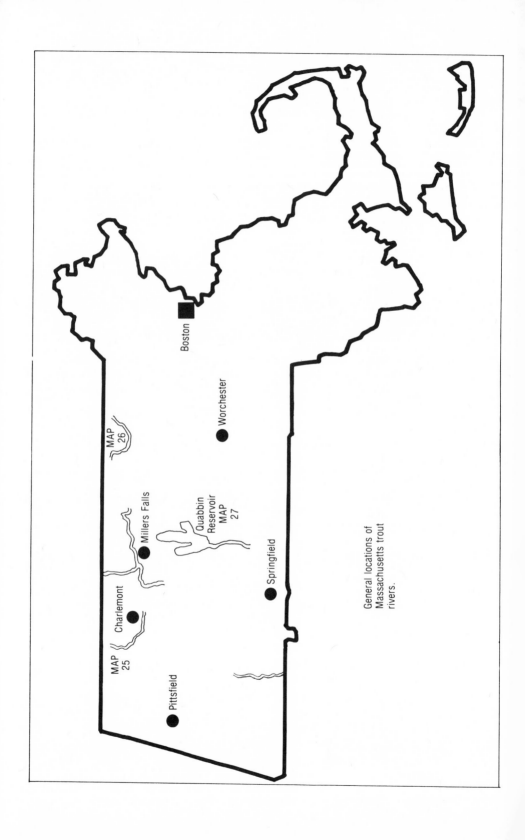

General locations of Massachusetts trout rivers.

Chapter 6

The Rivers of Massachusetts

The Commonwealth of Massachusetts is often overlooked by trout fishermen of New England. With Vermont and New Hampshire directly to the north, and Maine only a matter of hours away, little attention is given to those rivers of Massachusetts containing populations of brook trout, rainbow trout, and brown trout.

This is indeed unfortunate. Massachusetts offers such rivers as the Deerfield (in my mind, one of the finest trout waters in New England), the Swift River, the Nissitissit River, and the Green and Farington rivers. Each is unique, and provides good to high quality trout fishing possibilities.

Many rivers in Massachusetts did suffer from pollution in past decades, but that problem is now being dealt with successfully in many cases. The Nissitissit River is a prime example; only a few short years ago trout could not survive due to pollution, but today this river is far along on the road to recovery and provides some excellent trout fishing. The Nissitissit River even has a fly fishing only section, one of the few in the state.

To aid the recovery of several rivers, then with hopes of establishing permanent stocks, the Massachusetts Division of Fisheries and Wildlife conducts massive stocking programs in all sections of the state. Brown trout and rainbow trout are the principal species stocked on an annual basis, with a number of rivers also receiving brook trout.

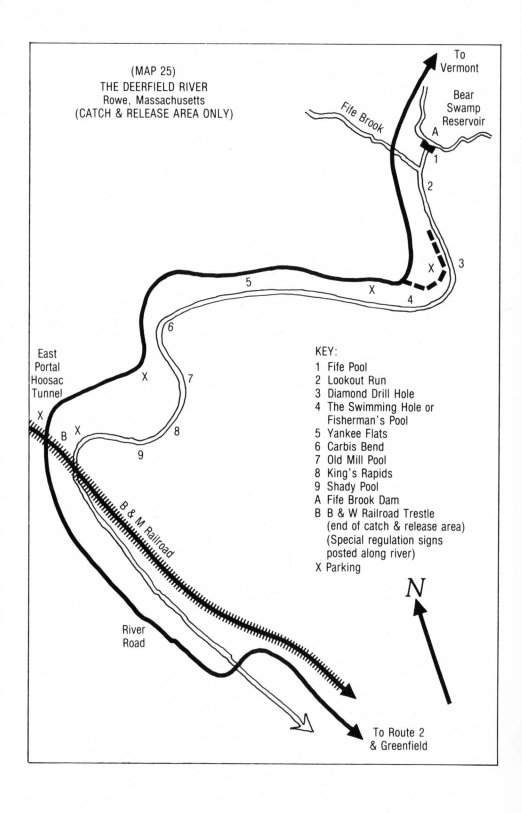

(MAP 25)
THE DEERFIELD RIVER
Rowe, Massachusetts
(CATCH & RELEASE AREA ONLY)

To Vermont

Bear Swamp Reservoir

Fife Brook

A

1
2
3
4
5
6
7
8
9

X
X
X

East Portal Hoosac Tunnel
X
B
X

B & M Railroad

River Road

KEY:
1 Fife Pool
2 Lookout Run
3 Diamond Drill Hole
4 The Swimming Hole or Fisherman's Pool
5 Yankee Flats
6 Carbis Bend
7 Old Mill Pool
8 King's Rapids
9 Shady Pool
A Fife Brook Dam
B B & W Railroad Trestle
  (end of catch & release area)
  (Special regulation signs posted along river)
X Parking

N

To Route 2 & Greenfield

THE DEERFIELD RIVER

Rowe
(Catch & Release Area Only)

GENERAL DESCRIPTION

Without question, the finest trout river which Massachusetts has to offer is the Deerfield River in the town of Rowe. Here is a most unique coldwater fishery that rivals many of New England's more renowned habitats, yet receives little acclaim or attention other than by resident fishermen and the few non-resident enthusiasts who know about it.

The Deerfield has its source in the rolling hill country of Dover, Vermont. It is blocked in the town of Whitingham, Vermont, by Harriman Dam (forming Lake Whitingham, a massive lake trout, brown trout, and rainbow trout habitat). It enters the State of Massachusetts at the town of Rowe, where it is blocked once again by Fife Brook Dam, which forms the huge Sherman Reservoir. It is below Fife Brook Dam where the special catch-and-release area starts, and where some highly productive and challenging trout water is found.

The catch-and-release area on the Deerfield River, so designated in 1979 after much effort by the Deerfield Valley Chapter of Trout Unlimited, stretches 1.6 miles downstream — and every bit of it is trout water. It is a mixture of deep pools, riffles, rapids, and moderately flowing water during periods of normal flow, while it is a mass of continuous whitewater and strong current during water release periods at Fife Brook Dam. The Deerfield (in this section) is not overly wide, and many of the better pools and riffle sections can be easily waded; it is, however, a freestone bottom, mixed with some boulders and rocks, and wading can be tricky!

BEST PLACES TO FISH

The catch-and-release area of the Deerfield is blessed with riffles and pools and excellent trout fishing will be found just about anywhere along it. However, many of the better known pools and riffle areas are named:

1) Fife Pool, located at the base of Fife Brook Dam. This is a deep pool with a powerful current, agitated by water rushing from the dam. Large browns up to five pounds have been taken here, as well as some impressive rainbow trout.

2) Lookout Run, a set of riffles with a challenging current, just below Fife Pool.

3) Diamond Drill Hole, an interesting pool with a set of riffles at both ends holding some hesitant rainbows and browns.

4) The Swimming Hole, located around the bend from Diamond Drill Hole (I've seen trout consistently rising in this pool but getting them to accept a fly is an ultimate challenge).

5) Yankee Flats, located approximately one-half mile below Fife Brook Dam, a set of magnificent riffles.

Other well-known fishing spots include Carbis Bend (6), the Old Mill Pool (7), Kings Rapids (8), and Shady Pool (located upstream from the B&M Railroad trestle).

BEST TIMES TO FISH

Excellent fishing is available on the catch-and-release area throughout the Massachusetts fishing season. There are some facts the fisherman should be aware of, however.

Water is released from Fife Brook Dam on a daily basis throughout the summer. Water levels within the release area rise exceedingly fast and fishermen should remember to keep an eye on the water level. Water is always released during the same period daily, shortly before 9 a.m. The best fishing throughout the season, therefore, is from daybreak to approximately this time each morning, or until levels are too high for feasible fishing.

Productive fishing comes back each afternoon when water outage from Fife Brook is shut down — the river reaches normal levels by 3 p.m. or 4 p.m., allowing excellent possibilities from that time to dusk.

This water release and daily fluctuation of the Deerfield's water level allows temperatures to be maintained within a comfortable range for trout — this, coupled with the river's many rapids, riffles, and deep pools, provides excellent fishing throughout the fishing season. If a fisherman is interested in peak periods, however, they are May, June, and early July, and again from September to the end of the season in October.

BEST FLIES

The Deerfield is rich in insect life; May fly and caddis fly species are well-represented, and hatches occur throughout much of the season. A recent stream study, conducted jointly by the Deerfield Chapter of Trout Unlimited and Northeast Utilities, discovered and documented over 30 subspecies of May fly, caddis fly, and other insects along the Deerfield River. Below are some of the most important, their emerging date, and suggested imitations:

SPECIES	IMITATION	HATCHING PERIOD
Ephemerella subvaria	Hendrickson, Red Quill, Lady Beaverkill	Mid-May to Early June
Ephemerella rotunda	Dark Red Quill	End of May to Mid-June
Ephemerella invaria	Dark Blue Winged Hendrickson	End of May to Mid-June
Ephemerella dorothea	Pale Evening Dun, Little Maryatt	Early June to Early July
Ephemerella lata	Blue Winged Olive, Light Blue Winged Olive	July to Mid-August
Ephemerella simplex	Dark Slate Winged Olive	Late June through September
Paraleptophlebia adoptiva	Blue Quill, Blue Dun, Iron Blue Dun	May
Ephemera guttulata	Green Drake	June
Stenonema	American March Brown, Ginger Quill, Light Cahill	June through August
Stenonema fuscum	Grey Fox, Ginger Quill	Late May to Early June
Epeorus	Quill Gordon, Iron Dun	Late May to Early July
Epeorus vitrea	Pale Evening Dun	Late May to Early June
Baetis	Blue Winged Olive	April - May

ORDER TRICOPTERA (caddis flies)

Hydropsyche		Early May; September
Macronema	Dark Green Caddis	Late May through June
Fuscula	Pale Olive Caddis	May and June

These and other flies are best tied on hook sizes 12 to 16.

Wet flies: Light Cahill, Ginger Quill, Quill Gordon, Female Beaver-kill, Light Hendrickson, Dark Hendrickson, March Brown, Leadwing Coachman, Blue Dun, Hare's Ear, and Iron Blue Dun (sizes 10 to 14).

GENERAL NOTES

The special catch-and-release area of the Deerfield River opens to fishing April 18, closing October 18. All fish must be immediately released to the river. Only artificial lures may be used.

Camping and lodging facilities will be found along Route 2 in Charle-mont. Recommended facilities include: The Oxbow Motel, Mohawk Trail, Charlemont, MA 01339, telephone (413) 625-6729; and Pike's Camping Area, Route 2, East Charlemont, MA 01370, telephone (413) 625-2996.

HOW TO REACH THE CATCH-AND-RELEASE AREA OF THE DEERFIELD RIVER

From eastern Massachusetts, take Route 2 west to Charlemont. Just before the Mohawk Memorial Bridge over the Deerfield River (2.2 miles west of Charlemont), turn right on Zoar Road. Drive 3.5 miles to a fork in the road and turn left, passing under a railroad underpass and over a bridge. 3.6 miles brings you to Hoosac Tunnel, where parking is available, and the B&M Railroad Trestle: this is the lower end of the catch-and-release area. Continue on to Fife Brook Dam and the upper end of the area.

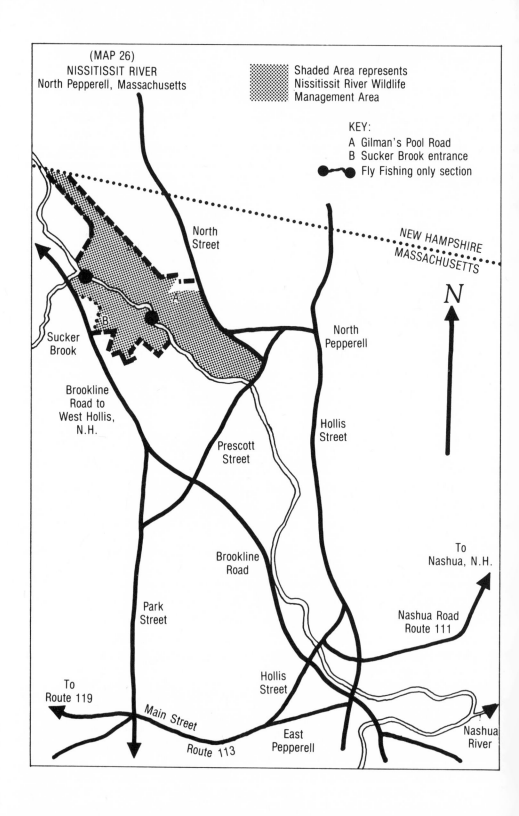

(MAP 26)
NISSITISSIT RIVER
North Pepperell, Massachusetts

Shaded Area represents
Nissitissit River Wildlife
Management Area

KEY:
A Gilman's Pool Road
B Sucker Brook entrance
Fly Fishing only section

NEW HAMPSHIRE
MASSACHUSETTS

N

North
Street

North
Pepperell

A

B

Sucker
Brook

Brookline
Road to
West Hollis,
N.H.

Prescott
Street

Hollis
Street

Brookline
Road

To
Nashua, N.H.

Park
Street

Nashua Road
Route 111

Hollis
Street

To
Route 119

Main Street

East
Pepperell

Nashua
River

Route 113

THE NISSITISSIT RIVER

North Pepperell

GENERAL DESCRIPTION

The Nissitissit River is one of the best trout fishing areas for browns in eastern Massachusetts. Until recently, it could not be considered such, but within the past few years great success has been achieved in making the Nissitissit a high-quality habitat for trout.

The river flows generally southward from Potanipo Pond in Brookline, New Hampshire. Its upper sections consist of riffles and pools — but once the Nissitissit enters Massachusetts, it slows in pace, widens, grows deeper, and takes on the characteristics of a small river. Some good trout fishing is available at specific times of the fishing season.

BEST PLACES TO FISH

The Nissitissit River flows from the New Hampshire/Massachusetts state boundary into the town of North Pepperell. It eventually enters the Nashua River at East Pepperell.

Unquestionably, the best trout section lies within the short fly-fishing-only area in North Pepperell. The section lies within the Nissitissit River Wildlife Management Area, a protected wooded tract of land lying between the Brookline Road in Pepperell and North Street in North Pepperell.

The fly-fishing-only area starts from where Sucker Brook enters the river and runs downstream approximately one and one-half miles to what is known as Gilma's Pool. This is generally slow to moderate flowing water with short riffle stretches.

BEST TIMES TO FISH

Early May through June; July in the early morning hours and late afternoon; September and October.

BEST FLIES

Wet flies: March Brown, Light Cahill, Female Beaverkill, Ginger

Quill, and other natural-colored sub-surface imitations, fished slowly with floating lines.

Dry flies: Adams, March Brown, Light Cahill, Hendrickson, Red Quill, Hare's Ear, Whirling Blue Dun, Pale Evening Dun, and Quill Gordon (sizes 12 to 16). Terrestrial imitations (sizes 14 to 16).

GENERAL NOTES

The Nissitissit River opens to fishing April 18, closing October 18. Special regulations may exist. Check Massachusetts abstracts of the fish and wildlife laws for updated limits and season variations. That section of the Nissitissit River from Sucker Brook downstream to Gilman's Pool is restricted to fly fishing only.

HOW TO REACH THE NISSITISSIT RIVER

From Lowell, take Route 113 to Pepperell.

From Portland, Maine, take the Maine Turnpike south to Kittery, then follow Interstate 95 to Interstate 495. Take 495 to Lowell, then take Route 113 to Pepperell.

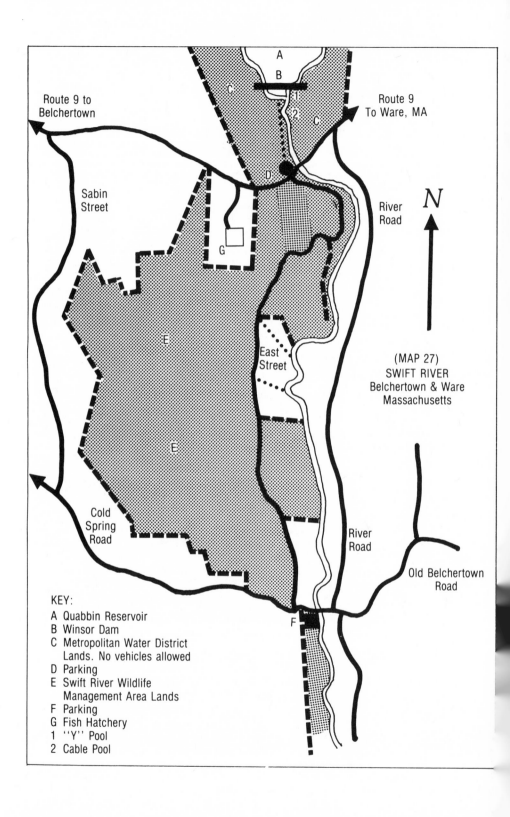

Route 9 to Belchertown

Route 9 To Ware, MA

Sabin Street

River Road

N

Cold Spring Road

East Street

River Road

Old Belchertown Road

(MAP 27)
SWIFT RIVER
Belchertown & Ware
Massachusetts

KEY:
A Quabbin Reservoir
B Winsor Dam
C Metropolitan Water District Lands. No vehicles allowed
D Parking
E Swift River Wildlife Management Area Lands
F Parking
G Fish Hatchery
1 ''Y'' Pool
2 Cable Pool

THE SWIFT RIVER

Belchertown, Massachusetts

GENERAL DESCRIPTION

The Swift River leaves the massive Quabbin Reservoir and travels southward, entering the Chicopee River at Three Rivers. It is an amazingly clean, cold river that provides some interesting, if not the highest quality, fishing opportunities for rainbow and brook trout. It is the best trout river in central Massachusetts. Fish average 8 to 11 inches, with 12- to 13-inch examples taken occasionally.

The Swift River is not wide. Because the water is so clear, however, careful wading and presentation of the fly are musts if action is to be expected. The river is well-bordered by trees, providing shade and protective cover. Insect life is not overly strong, although the Swift does experience both May fly and caddis fly activity.

BEST PLACES TO FISH

The fly-fishing-only section, which stretches one mile downstream from Winsor Dam to the bridge on Route 9, offers the best trout fishing. Limited success is also possible downstream from Route 9 as far as the Spring Road.

BEST TIMES TO FISH

Like the Deerfield River, water flow on the Swift River is regulated daily by Winsor Dam. Water is released around 7 a.m. each day — thus, the best fishing is found from sun-up to about that time. This fluctuation, however, keeps the water temperature at a consistent 50- to 55-degree average throughout the fishing season, providing excellent trout fshing right through the season, even during the summer.

Water levels recede by late afternoon. The fisherman should concentrate his time on the Swift River between the hours of sun-up to approximately 7 a.m., and during the afternoon, throughout the season.

BEST FLIES

Wet flies: Woolly Worms, Light Cahill, Hendrickson, March Brown, Hare's Ear, Leadwing Coachman, Picket Pin, Blue Dun, Iron Blue Dun, Ginger Quill, and Female Beaverkill (sizes 10 to 14).

Dry flies: Adams, March Brown, Light Cahill, Hendrickson, Henryville Special, Hairwing Caddis, Hare's Ear, and Gray Fox (sizes 12 to 16).

GENERAL NOTES

The Swift River opens to fishing April 18. It closes October 18. The daily creel limit is six fish. That section of the Swift River from Winsor Dam downstream to Route 9 is restricted to fly fishing only.

HOW TO REACH THE SWIFT RIVER

From eastern Massachusetts and Maine points, take Massachusetts Route 2 west to North New Salem, then take Route 202 south to Belchertown. Go east on Route 9 from Belchertown to the bridge over the Swift River. Parking is available at the bridge, and a foot trail leads along the river to Winsor Dam.

ACKNOWLEDGEMENTS

Many thanks and much appreciation is given to the following individuals who gave freely of their time, homes, and knowledge during the compilation of this book:

Maine — to fellow fly fishing enthusiasts Ron Masure, owner of the Leisure Life Lodge in Greenville; John Nichols of Oquossoc, and Wilmot "Wiggie" Robinson of Millinocket for their assistance in naming the many pools on the Roach, Kennebago, and West Branch Penobscot rivers, respectively.

New Hampshire — to Robert (Bob) Harris of Goffstown for putting a roof over my head and food in my belly and for guiding me on the Contoocook, Souhegan, and Little Sugar rivers; and to Dr. Fred Giamo of Peterborough for his assistance on the Contoocook.

Massachusetts — to Frank Sousa and Bill (Buffalo) Borchers (and families) for making our trip to the Bay State so memorable and productive; and to Herm Prillips, owner of the Oxbow Motel in Charlemont for putting us up while we fished the magnificent Deerfield River.

And finally, to the Maine Department of Inland Fisheries and Wildlife, and New Hampshire Fish and Game Department, the Vermont Fish and Game Department, and the Massachusetts Division of Fisheries and Game for providing much helpful information and data on request.

NORTH COUNTRY PRESS

Outdoor and Nature Guides

Katahdin
A Guide to Baxter State Park and Mount Katahdin
by Stephen Clark
From his long experience of the Park, author Clark has assembled a complete reference in a handy, pocket-sized package. Featured are detailed descriptions of all access points, trails, and campsites, plus a guide to the Park's flora and fauna, and more.
17 × 23 inch map, photos, 224 pp. $8.95

Pocket Guide to the Maine Outdoors
by Eben Thomas
Here is a wealth of information about the Maine outdoors in one compact, but thorough, volume. Included are the 20 top canoe trips in Maine, top hiking trails, and listings for literally hundreds of outdoors resources, activities, and organizations, including state parks, campgrounds, hunting, fishing, snowmobiling, and much more.
Maps, charts, photos, 256 pp. $9.95

Bassin' in New England
by William Chauvin and Carl Apperson
Let Bill and Carl be your guides to the most enjoyable and productive black bass waters New England has to offer. Includes state by state recommendations of *specific* waters, and tips on safety, equipment, and techniques for beginning and advanced anglers alike.
Hardcover, maps, photos, 176 pp. $15.95

Fly Fishing in Maine
by Al Raychard
This is the most comprehensive, complete, and detailed guide to some of the best fishing available in the continental United States. Includes special chapters on Atlantic salmon and sea run brown trout, and specific where-to-go recommendations.
Maps, charts, photos, 176 pp. $7.95

Remote Trout Ponds in Maine
by Al Raychard
Over 60 drive-in (4WD recommended) or hike-in backcountry ponds are covered in this useful guide. Seasonal water levels and temperatures are covered, as well as timing of the peak hatches. A must for adventurous anglers seeking new, uncrowded, and unspoiled waters!
Maps, 212 pp. $7.95

The Allagash
by Lew Dietz
This classic volume covers the whole of the great Allagash Wilderness, from the early days of the map makers and Abnaki Indians to its present status as one of the last truly wild rivers in the East.
Maps, illustrations, 256 pp. $8.95

Look for these fine selections at your bookstore, or call us at 800-223-6121 (outside of Maine) or 207-948-2962 (in state) for further information or to order.